# The Revived Life

# THE
# REVIVED
# LIFE

Lewis A. Drummond

**BROADMAN PRESS**
Nashville, Tennessee

© Copyright 1982 ● Broadman Press.
All rights reserved.

4252-05
ISBN: 0-8054-5205-2

Dewey Decimal Classification: 248
Subject heading: SPIRITUAL LIFE
Library of Congress Catalog Card Number: 82-71217

Printed in the United States of America

Dedicated to

## Dr. and Mrs. Duke K. McCall

*Their lives have been dedicated to the spiritual enrichment of others. God has used them to awaken and inspire countless Christians to reach their potential under Jesus Christ. They have exemplified in their lives the motto of the seminary they have so ably served: "That the man of God may be perfect, throughly furnished unto all good works" (2 Tim. 3:17, KJV).*

# Foreword

We are all familiar with the heart cry for revival that reverberates through the Holy Scriptures—"revive thy work" (Hab. 3:2, KJV); "revive us" (Ps. 85:6, KJV); and "revive me" (Ps. 138:7, KJV). This book is concerned with the last of these symbolic phrases, "revive me."

It is so easy to listen to stories of great revivals, or even to lecture on the mighty awakenings of the Spirit through the centuries, and yet be *personally* unaffected. In fact, it has been my experience that even talking about the subject can often be an excuse for dodging the individual issues that must be faced in revival.

Norman Grubb, in his little book *Continuous Revival*, testifies to this danger. It was not until he visited the East Central Africa revival in 1950 that something "transforming" happened in his life. He writes:

> It has meant a new discovery by me and many others of what we mean by "revival." When we come down to it in simplest form, it means the re-viving of dead areas in our lives. I remember when I first heard two [brothers] from Ruanda speaking very quietly and simply for two days in our London headquarters to about ninety of our staff. At the last meeting, they very quietly opened the door for any present to say anything that was on their hearts. Very soon one and another were bringing to the light areas in their lives where they had come face to face with sin unobserved by them before and were bringing them to the cleansing blood. I got a real shock at the end when one of the two quietly said, "I

don't know if you realize it, friends, but this is revival." The transforming truth of that statement took time to sink in and is still sinking in! It began to shake me out of the misconception of years, that revival could only come in great soul-shaking outpourings of the Spirit. Thank God for such when they do come; they have been the great and precious hurricanes of the Spirit in the history of the Church. . . . But now I see that "revival" in its truest sense is an everyday affair right down within the reach of everyday folk to be experienced in our hearts, homes and churches, and in our fields of service.[1]

In a similar vein, I recall being challenged profoundly by the Reverend Duncan Campbell. It was the height of the Northern Hebrides revival (1951), and Campbell was in London for medical treatment. His voice had given out with the strain of continuous preaching. My wife and I were honored to entertain him in our parsonage. Needless to say, we wanted a firsthand report of what God was doing in the Highlands of Scotland, and, bless his heart, our guest did his best to inform us. But then he paused and looked into our faces and said in a hoarse whisper, "Don't let the Hebrides revival rob you of a personal revival!"

A study of the revivals of the past makes it clear that there is a distinction between revival with a capital R and revival with a small r. There are times when God in his sovereignty sweeps through a church, community, or country like "a rushing mighty wind." People are caught up in the movement of the Spirit irresistibly and inexplicably. In other words, there are mysterious phenomena in revival, but equally important is the fact that God uses the human element. Dr. Louis King has pointed out that the Bible and history "reveal that there has never been such a thing as a prayerless revival."

So with the capital R there is the small r, and that is where you and I come in. God has to begin somewhere, with someone. First, he enlists the individual, but then he proceeds to establish the remnant, or what Dr. Vance Havner calls "God's kindling wood." Thus revival is initially and essentially personal. And it is to this aspect of revival that Dr. Lewis A. Drummond addresses himself in this excellent volume. With a concise and yet comprehensive treatment, he deals with the successive and progressive ways in which God deals with his people. From the author's perspective, this book logically follows his previous work, *The Awakening That Must Come* (Broadman Press). I, therefore, most warmly welcome and commend *The Revived Life* to every Christian who means business with God. Here is a book which will lead the pastors and members of our churches into "the full measure of the blessing of Christ" (Rom. 15:29, NIV).

There is nothing for which I preach and pray more fervently than for a heaven-sent revival in our time. So I urge all who prayerfully read these pages to apply *personally* the truths that are so clearly set forth, and then sing from the heart:

> O Holy Spirit, revival comes from thee;
> Send a revival, start the work in me.
> (J. Edwin Orr, "Search Me, O God")

STEPHEN F. OLFORD
President, Encounter Ministries, Inc.
Wheaton, Illinois

# Preface

The excitement of a new, fresh Great Awakening swirls in the air. Everywhere God's people are talking about a coming spiritual revival. More important, burdened prayer groups for a mighty moving of the Holy Spirit are springing up across the land. Discerning Christians are convinced God is about to do something not seen for many years and are earnestly praying to that end. That we need an outpouring of God's power and presence is obvious to all. The insightful see it just about to burst on the scene.

In my last book, *The Awakening That Must Come*, I outlined the principles and history of Great Awakenings. Since its publication, however, I have become increasingly convinced that a volume is needed that emphasizes the personal, individual aspects of a spiritual revival. Although there was an element of personal challenge in my first work, a book that dealt in detail with personal principles of revival seemed relevant. With this in mind, I present my second work on spiritual awakening. The thrust is personal, individual, and practical. It attempts to answer the basic questions on *how* to have a personal revival. It is hoped that, being revived, Christians can then take their places in God's plan to precipitate a general Great Awakening. If that divine scheme can in any way be aided by this volume, all my efforts in writing will be amply repaid. In the preparation of *The Revived Life* I have adapted a few relevant passages from *Leading Your Church in Evangelism* and *The Awakening That Must Come*, both published by Broadman Press, and from *Life Can Be Real*, published in England in 1973.

I must express my debt to those whose efforts have been invaluable to the production of this book. The tireless workers in Office Services at The Southern Baptist Theological Seminary, Louisville, Kentucky, deserve my gratitude. They did the manuscript typing in a sacrificial and professional manner. To my wife, Betty, who always does her matchless work as proofreader, I express deep appreciation.

My prayer attends this small book that God may use it in your life to help revive you and that in turn the Holy Spirit may use you to revive a very needy world.

# Contents

O Holy Spirit, revival comes from thee;
Send a revival, start the work in me.
Thy Word declares thou wilt supply our need;
For blessings now, O Lord, I humbly plead.
(J. Edwin Orr, "Search Me, O God")

> For lo, the winter is past,
> the rain is over and gone.
> The flowers appear on the earth,
> the time of singing has come.
> (Song of Solomon 2:11-12*a*)

# 1
# The Revived Life Is an Awakened Life

The lush, verdant Rhondda Valley of South Wales had never witnessed anything like it before. Electric excitement crackled in the charged atmosphere. Everyone was aghast, from the rugged miners black with coal dust as they shot up the shafts after a shift in the bowels of the earth to the sedate little ladies over a cup of afternoon tea. Groups gathered on street corners to wrestle with the strange happenings in their normally quiet part of Britain. It was the topic of conversations in shops, factories, schools—everywhere people spoke of nothing else. You could not turn around without bumping into the affair. Newspapers were replete with reports. Had they had television in 1904—that's the time frame of the phenomenon—every newscast would have been crammed with commentaries on the strange event. Wales was turned on and alive as seldom seen. History was being made.

## The Welsh Revival

The conflagration had been ignited in a theological school, of all places. A small Welsh pastor's training institution was the scene where the spark was first struck. Evangelist Seth Joshua had been invited by the school authorities to speak to the ministerial students. Nothing was unusual about that. Special lectures are part and parcel of a theological education. During one of Joshua's messages, the evangelist struck the theme of doing God's will. In the course of his sermon he said, "God could mightily use any person whom he could *bend* to His will." Many were mightily moved. Involved in the service on that occasion was a minister, twenty-six-year-old Evan Roberts, a fine young student. The preacher's words fell like a bludgeoning hammer on Roberts's sensitive soul. In deep distress, he sank to his knees and from a crushed conscience cried, "O God, *bend* me!" God bent him. Then lifting him up, the Holy Spirit through his young, bent servant began a movement for Christ and righteousness that put Wales in a spiritual spiral like it had never seen before—or since. The great Welsh revival of 1904-1906 was launched.

Evan Roberts, with others, had been earnestly praying for their beloved country for some time. The spiritual sterility of Wales as the twentieth century emerged on the scene was overwhelming. Queen Victoria and her age had died; the church had seemed to die with her. So Roberts prayed and prayed that God would revive his work. And through the young preacher, God did just that.

Those dynamic days stagger the most stable historians. One would have said it was impossible that such things as were regularly occurring could actually take place. It seemed that the whole countryside was resurrected from the depth of secularity to the delights of spirituality in a single stroke of the Spirit.

The churches all up and down the Valley, and finally over the entire nation, were jammed to overflowing twenty-four hours a day, seven days a week. Singing, preaching, rejoicing, conversions, and newness abounded everywhere. As the miners spilled out of the collieries they bathed and went directly to their chapel, many to stay most of the night. There was no problem gathering people to church. It seemed the whole population was there.

Some rather humorous episodes were actually recorded during these exciting times. The production problem that emerged in the mines as a result of the revival is a case in point. The Rhondda Valley of South Wales is a coal-mining district and a rich source of energy. At the turn of the twentieth century, modern mechanization had not been brought into the mines. Coal had to be drawn out of the deep shafts by horses. Prior to the awakening, the animals heard their commands punctuated with cursing. The Welsh miners were, for the most part, a pretty rough lot. So many of the miners were converted and their language cleaned up, the horses did not know how to work. The animals literally had to be taken out of the mines and retrained. That was a "blessed slowdown" of production, as one person put it.

An example of the sheer power of the movement comes from a public school. As the revival fires blazed, a young boy in one of the local schools became very agitated about his relationship to Jesus Christ. The teacher, realizing the problem, told the lad he could go home and sent him accompanied by an older Christian boy. As they made their way to the house, they passed an abandoned building. The concerned student suggested they go inside and pray. They entered, fell on their knees, and it was not long until the lad was rejoicing—having opened up his life to the Lord Jesus.

With the joy of salvation bubbling in his heart, the boy was bursting to share with his classmates. They ran back to the school, flew into the classroom, and the new believer blurted out, "Jesus Christ has saved me." As these words filled the air, deep conviction took hold of the entire class. One by one, the other boys got up without permission and went outside. Soon the room was emptied. Their teacher was appalled. Welsh pupils did not do that in 1904.

When the teacher recovered from his astonishment, he too went outside to see what had happened to his students. There even greater astonishment gripped him, for he found the lads on their knees by the side of the school building, weeping and crying to God for mercy that they might find the forgiveness of sins.

Soon their prayers permeated the other classes of boys on the first floor. With their cries came conviction, and soon the entire first floor was on its knees pleading aloud for mercy. The girls were taught in classrooms on the second floor. As they heard the heartbreaking prayers of the boys below, they too fell deeply under the Spirit's power, and in a matter of moments they also were agonizing for forgiveness.

It was not long, of course, before the parents and the townspeople got the report. They rushed to the school to see what was happening to their children. The moment they crossed the threshold of the building, however, they were immediately smitten with deep conviction. In a matter of hours, practically the entire community came to Christ. It was quite incredible. Yet, this kind of phenomenon was almost typical. Conversions were counted in tens, even hundreds, of thousands. The old believers were renewed and filled with such an influx of new, divine life that everyone and everything seemed radically altered. God was everywhere.

Civic and social righteousness swept in like a flood. The jails emptied; the pubs closed; the dance halls shut their doors; the entire country was transformed. At that time in Wales, if no crimes were being committed the judges wore white gloves to signify the fact there were no cases to try. All the magistrates were so clothed. What were the police to do in such a crimeless country? They hit upon a solution; the officers organized themselves into singing groups and made themselves available to the churches. The Welsh people have always been a great singing people. Music was, therefore, a very central element in the new thrust of the Spirit. Thus the "bobbies" found a job.

## A Vital Principle Emerges

No denomination was exempt from the movement. The Church of Wales, the Presbyterians, the Baptists—all were caught up in the blessed time. What a day for those fortunate people! And it all began when one young Christian man permitted God to "bend" him. That is the way it always is. God uses those who are yielded to his will. That is the prime point. Evan Roberts's experience should not, of course, be judged on its emotional content or immediate circumstances, as dramatic as they were. That is never the issue. The principle is, Roberts simply let God have complete control of his life. The committed will is the bottom line to an awakening, personal or national. In a word, through a life surrendered to the Savior, the Holy Spirit can do great things. One revived life can be used by God to do marvelous works, maybe even the changing of the entire course of a country. That is a tremendous thought—and a significant principle.

## The Eighteenth Century Awakening

In 1738, the Spirit of God was probing deep in Britain. Joy began to abound all over London. Many had found Christ. There was one very disturbed young man, however. Even though he was a minister of the gospel, he had no joy, no peace, no spiritual reality in his life. Then on Wednesday, May 24, 1738, something occurred that radically altered everything. He recorded the fascinating event in his journal:

> In the evening I went very unwillingly to a society in Aldersgate Street, where one was reading Luther's preface to the *Epistle to the Romans*. About a quarter before nine, while he was describing the change which God works in the heart through faith in Christ, I felt my heart strangely warmed. I felt I did trust in Christ, Christ alone for salvation; and an assurance was given me that He had taken away *my* sins, even *mine*, and saved *me* from the law of sin and death. I began to pray with all my might for those who had in a more especial manner despitefully used me and persecuted me. I then testified openly to all there what I now first felt in my heart.[1]

A man was born again. Not only was a man born anew; a nation was about to be vitally changed. Aldersgate had come.

The man? John Wesley. The nation? Britain. The great eighteenth century awakening, conceived in the grace of God, was ready for its birth through the ministry of this unusual man who met Christ at the simple Aldersgate society meeting.

It had been a long, languishing, and at times very lonely struggle for John. The birth pains had begun at Oxford University where as a student he and his brother Charles and friend George Whitefield had joined the "Holy Club." The trio wanted to know God, really know him. And though they struggled and strove, no satisfaction came. So methodical were they in their pursuit of God and holiness that they were dubbed "Methodists"—a derogatory phrase in those days.

After university days, Whitefield had a profound salvation experience of Jesus Christ and immediately launched a zealous ministry of evangelism and social action. George went to America to preach and institute an orphanage. He soon called his friend John to join him in the New World endeavor.

Both the Wesley brothers went to the colonies. Perhaps a

fresh start in a new place would help. But even there John was met with discouragement. The orphanage work went fairly well, but the "conversion of the heathen"—as they would have expressed it in those days—never got off the ground. Moreover, the primitive culture of the American Indians and the ruggedness of Savannah, Georgia, were radically different from the genteel atmosphere that would normally surround an Oxford Anglican priest in sophisticated London. Yet, that was not the real problem. Any dedicated man of God can suffer hardship and endure cultural shock *if* he has something to give to that difficult culture. That was the problem; John had nothing to give, not even anything to say. As a defeated, discouraged, depressed man he set sail for the homeland and penned in his diary, "I went to America to convert the heathen, but, O, who will convert me?"

Strange, isn't it? A man of the church, a graduate in religion of a great university, a soul in a sincere search for God and holiness, dedicated to the ministry, struggling and striving earnestly, yet not knowing God and feeling sick in his very spirit! But John was tenacious if nothing else; he would not stop seeking peace with Jesus Christ.

Back in London, a Moravian minister by the name of Peter Bohler crossed the Wesley brothers' path. Bohler had come out of the great Moravian revival that broke on the estate of Count Ludwig von Zinzendorf in Herrnhut, Germany. He was filled with zeal and fire for Christ. He knew the Lord and the glorious gospel very well indeed. He helped John and his brother Charles tremendously.

Soon Charles Wesley grasped a confident conviction in Christ as personal Savior. George Whitefield had been preaching with profound effect for two years. Now John was all alone in his struggle. The pressure was building up and becoming almost unbearable. He *must* find Christ and salvation—yet he *must* do it with honesty and integrity.

It was then, on that fateful night, he reluctantly went to the meeting on Aldersgate Street. What a night! Aldersgate will always be remembered in Methodist circles. John Wesley had experienced Jesus Christ as Lord and Savior. He was saved, and the Spirit of God took up his divine residence in John's life. That is invariably the beginning of it all. God can do nothing through a person until that person becomes a true born-again believer.

But *no sweeping revival came at that moment*, at least through John Wesley. The full awakening did not break at Aldersgate Street, although that was John's beginning. In fact, it was some nine months before the true tidal wave of the Spirit was ready to deluge the land through this servant of Christ. There is an often overlooked excerpt in John Wesley's journal that cries to be heard afresh. The time was New Year's morning, 1739. Wesley recorded:

> Mr. Hall, Kinchin, Ingham, Whitefield, Hutchins, and my brother Charles were present at our love feast in Fetter Lane, with about sixty of our brethren. About three in the morning, as we were continuing instant in prayer, the power of God came mightily upon us, insomuch that many cried out for exceeding joy, and many fell to the ground. As soon as we were recovered a little from that awe and amazement at the presence of His Majesty we broke out with one voice, "We praise Thee, O God; we acknowledge Thee to be the Lord."[2]

The Fetter Lane "little pentecost" as history calls it, had come; and the revival that had really already begun now began to spread with ever increasing momentum and power. The Holy Spirit had come in power, and the great Wesley-Whitefield awakening moved forward.

Let it be understood, to be scripturally precise Wesley had already been converted when the so-called "little pentecost" of Fetter Lane occurred. That was the meaning of his Aldersgate experience. Therefore, John already possessed the indwelling

Holy Spirit, as do all genuine believers. This principle will be brought out clearly in a later chapter. Therefore, for history to term the Fetter Lane event a "pentecost" is really a bit of a misnomer. That must be granted, for the Pentecost experience recorded in the second chapter of Acts cannot be repeated, at least in the historical sense. On that day, God once and for all poured out his blessed Spirit on the church. It is no more repeatable—in principle, that is—than the cross or resurrection of our Lord Jesus Christ. Yet, Christians live and are sustained daily on the benefits of the cross, resurrection, and the outpouring of the Spirit on the Day of Pentecost. That is why historians called Wesley's Fetter Lane experience a "little pentecost." And in that sense they are quite correct. Thus, what actually happened to Wesley at the Fetter Lane prayer meeting was a refreshing, a reviving, and infilling of God's Spirit that blessed, challenged, encouraged, empowered, and thrust him out in great evangelistic activity. He was awakened anew. He was personally revived.

All great movements of God to revive society have something of that pattern. Before God can use a believer in a great way, that believer must be filled with the Spirit. This truth can be documented historically over and over again. No competent church historian or Bible scholar can deny that obvious fact of the Scriptures and history. Dig deep enough, and it is always there. This shall become increasingly clear as we proceed.

What an awakening Britain had! Space forbids any adequate tabulating of that tremendous time. Multiplied volumes have set out the events of those great days. Hundreds of thousands were converted. The Methodist church was born. Open-air evangelism was inaugurated. The wickedness and social evils of the day—it was an unbelievably licentious society in which Wesley and Whitefield were born—were all but laid to rest. Great reforms were effected. New social institutions came to life. England, Scotland, and Wales were so radically altered religiously and socially that many historians believe that the Eighteenth Century Awakening saved Britain from the bloody fate that racked almost to ruin eighteenth century France.

America had its touch, too. Writings on the awakening soon arrived on the shores of the New World. George Whitefield traveled to the colonies seven times and significantly impacted people all the way from Benjamin Franklin to the scholarly Jonathan Edwards. His preaching was magnificent. Franklin thought him to be the most effective public speaker alive. His voice was fantastic; he could be clearly heard and understood by a crowd of thirty thousand people in the open air with no amplification. He actually spoke to that many on several occasions. The famous British actor David Garrick said Whitefield could reduce an audience to tears by merely speaking the word "Mesopotamia." He was the real catalyst of the First Great Awakening in the colonies. Some writers contend he was the true father of the British Methodist revival. What a man! What a day! What a moving of God! What a revival!

## The Principle Emerges Again

Do you see the prime principle in this powerful movement that immediately surfaces again? The foundational fact is that the movement began with a believer getting thoroughly refreshed by God and becoming entirely open to the Holy Spirit's leading. Aldersgate recorded Wesley's conversion, but the Fetter Lane prayer meeting recorded the challenging and empowering of Wesley and Whitefield for the task. Revival begins with a revived life; that is the point of it all. Make no mistake; that is the way it has always been throughout Christian history. Examples are the great Franciscan Revival under Saint Francis in the thirteenth century, the Florentine Revival under Savonarola in the fifteenth century, and Jonathan Edwards and the First Great Awakening in America. Renewed lives can change a home, a church, perhaps at times an entire nation.

## The Finney Revival

The scene shifts to America and focuses on a little city nestled in western New York State in the year 1821. Studying in the law offices of Squire Benjamin Wright in Adams, New York was a brilliant, energetic, ambitious, but religiously critical young apprentice. The eager young lawyer had determined to hack out a successful law career in the western emigration exodus. Succeed he would; he had all the equipment. And he would never be hampered by being overly religious; actually, he understood virtually nothing about the Christian faith. It has been said of this young man that he was a splendid pagan—a young man rejoicing in his strength, proudly conscious of his physical and intellectual superiority to all around him. He stood six feet, two inches tall, and weighed 185 pounds. He was an imposing man.

Adams knew this young scintillating lawyer for his athletic ability and love of dancing. His influence was tremendous among the young people, who regarded him as their leader and hero. He was quite well educated for his day, possessing a knowledge of Latin, Greek, Hebrew, and music. But his blasé attitude towards religion predominated above all the other facets of his fascinating personality. Up until this time, he had not owned a copy of the Bible. It was not that he disbelieved the Scriptures, he just knew nothing about them—or had very little interest in them. He himself admitted later that he was "as ignorant of religion as a heathen." His name: Charles Grandison Finney.

The paradox was that in spite of his religious attitudes, Finney was choir director in the local Presbyterian church. He was quite a skilled musician; he not only played the cello beautifully but was adept at choral conducting as well. As choir director, Finney had to listen Sunday after Sunday to the hyper-Calvinistic preaching of his pastor, the Reverend George W. Gale. His only reaction was that Gale didn't make much sense.

The prayer meetings at Adams Presbyterian Church were even more of a problem to the young lawyer. For some strange reason, he attended regularly. There he endured the church's incessant interceding for a "revival of religion," as they expressed it. They prayed continually to that end, yet nothing of any significance seemed to happen. Finney became very skeptical of the praying congregation. One day he said rather bluntly, "You pray for revival, but you do not seem to expect a revival of religion to come." One must give credit to the young man; he was honest, if not very gracious.

This scene was repeated for some time in Finney's well-ordered life. Slowly, however, the critic began to sense a rather disturbing discontent. He started asking himself some probing questions. Did he really need God, even though things were shaping up very nicely for him? Was there truth to the gospel that Gale was gladly declaring, even if it did not appear to take much effect in people's lives? Were these Christians sincere, regardless of the fact that their prayers were seemingly unanswered? Was there something to it after all? Were his criticisms really valid? He began to take an honest look at himself. After all, he was taking an honest look at the professing believers of Adams, why not himself?

This consciousness of need continued to deepen until the crisis came. Then—well, Finney must be allowed to tell it in his own words. The story of Charles's conversion stands as a classic. In his autobiography he wrote:

On a Sabbath evening in the autumn of 1821, I made up my mind that I would settle the question of my soul's salvation at

once, that if it were possible I would make my peace with God.
. . . I carried this resolution into execution as sternly and
thoroughly as I could. I was, however, obliged to be a good deal in
the office. But as the providence of God would have it, I was not
much occupied either on Monday or Tuesday; and had opportunity to read my Bible and engage in prayer most of the time.

But I was very proud. . . . I was very unwilling to have any one
know that I was seeking the salvation of my soul. When I prayed I
would only whisper my prayer, after having stopped the key-hole
to the door, lest some one should discover that I was engaged in
prayer. Before that time I had my Bible lying on the table with the
law-books; and it never had occurred to me to be ashamed of
being found reading it, any more than I should be ashamed of
being found reading any of my other books.

But after I had addressed myself in earnest to the subject of my
own salvation, I kept my Bible, as much as I could, out of sight. If
I was reading it when anybody came in, I would throw my law-
books upon it, to create the impression that I had not had it in my
hand. . . . I did not want to see my minister, because I did not
want to let him know how I felt, and I had no confidence that he
would understand my case, and give me the direction that I
needed. . . . I felt myself shut up to the Bible.

During Monday and Tuesday my convictions increased; but
still it seemed as if my heart grew harder. I could not shed a tear; I
could not pray. I had no opportunity to pray above my breath;
and frequently I felt, that if I could be alone where I could use my
voice and let myself out, I should find relief in prayer. . . .

Tuesday night I had become very nervous; and in the night a
strange feeling came over me as if I was about to die. I knew that if
I did I should sink down to hell; but I quieted myself as best I
could until morning.

At an early hour I started for the office. But just before I arrived
at the office, something seemed to confront me with questions
like these: indeed, it seemed as if the inquiry was within myself,
as if an inward voice said to me, "What are you waiting for? Did
you not promise to give your heart to God? And what are you
trying to do? Are you endeavoring to work out a righteousness of
your own?"

Just at this point the whole question of Gospel salvation opened
to my mind in a manner most marvellous to me at the time. I

think I then saw, as clearly as I ever have in my life, the reality and fulness of the atonement of Christ. I saw that his work was a finished work; and that instead of having, or needing, any righteousness of my own to recommend me to God, I had to submit myself to the righteousness of God through Christ. Gospel salvation seemed to me to be an offer of something to be accepted; and that it was full and complete; and that all that was necessary on my part, was to get my own consent to give up my sins, and accept Christ. . . .

North of the village, and over a hill, lay a piece of woods, in which I was in the almost daily habit of walking, more or less, when it was pleasant weather. It was now October, and the time was past for my frequent walks there. Nevertheless, instead of going to the office, I turned and bent my course toward the woods, feeling that I must be alone, and away from all human eyes and ears, so that I could pour out my prayer to God.

But still my pride must show itself. As I went over the hill, it occurred to me that some one might see me and suppose that I was going away to pray. . . . I skulked along under the fence, till I got so far out of sight that no one from the village could see me. I then penetrated into the woods, I should think, a quarter of a mile, went over on the other side of the hill, and found a place where some large trees had fallen across each other, leaving an open place between. There I saw I could make a kind of closet. I crept into this place and knelt down for prayer. As I turned to go up into the woods, I recollect to have said, "I will give my heart to God, or I never will come down from there." I recollect repeating this as I went up—"I will give my heart to God before I ever come down again."

But when I attempted to pray I found that my heart would not pray. I had supposed that if I could only be where I could speak aloud, without being overheard, I could pray freely. But lo! when I came to try, I was dumb; that is, I had nothing to say to God; or at least I could say but a few words, and those without heart. In attempting to pray I would hear a rustling in the leaves, as I thought, and would stop and look up to see if somebody were not coming. This I did several times.

Finally I found myself verging fast to despair. I said to myself, "I cannot pray. My heart is dead to God, and will not pray." I then reproached myself for having promised to give my heart to God

before I left the woods. When I came to try, I found I could not
give my heart to God. . . . I began to feel deeply that it was too
late; that it must be that I was given up of God and was past hope.
. . . A great sinking and discouragement came over me, and I
felt almost too weak to stand upon my knees.

Just at this moment I again thought I heard some one approach
me, and I opened my eyes to see whether it were so. But right
there the revelation of my pride of heart, as the great difficulty
that stood in the way, was distinctly shown to me. An overwhelming sense of wickedness in being ashamed to have a human being
see me on my knees before God, took such powerful possession
of me, that I cried at the top of my voice, and exclaimed that I
would not leave that place if all the men on earth and all the devils
in hell surrounded me. "What!" I said, "such a degraded sinner as
I am, on my knees confessing my sins to the great and holy God;
and ashamed to have any human being, and a sinner like myself,
find me on my knees endeavoring to make my peace with my
offended God!" The sin appeared awful, infinite. It broke me
down before the Lord.

Just at that point this passage of Scripture seemed to drop into
my mind with a flood of light: "Then shall ye go and pray unto
me, and I will hearken unto you. Then shall ye seek me and find
me, when ye shall search for me with all your heart." I instantly
seized hold of this with my heart. I had intellectually believed the
Bible before; but never had the truth been in my mind that faith
was a voluntary trust instead of an intellectual state. I was as
conscious as I was of my existence, of trusting at that moment in
God's veracity. . . . I cried to Him, "Lord, I take thee at thy word.
Now thou knowest that I do search for thee with all my heart, and
that I have come here to pray to thee; and thou hast promised to
hear me."

. . . The Spirit seemed to lay stress upon that idea in the text,
"When you search for me with all your heart." The question of
when, that is of the present time, seemed to fall heavily into my
heart. I told the Lord that I should take him at his word; that he
could not lie; and that therefore I was sure that he heard my
prayer, and that he would be found of me.

He then gave me many other promises, both from the Old and
the New Testament, especially some most precious promises
respecting our Lord Jesus Christ. I never can, in words, make any

human being understand how precious and true those promises appeared to me. I took them one after the other as infallible truth, the assertions of God who could not lie. They did not seem so much to fall into my intellect as into my heart, to be put within the grasp of the voluntary powers of my mind; and I seized hold of them, appropriated them, and fastened upon them with the grasp of a drowning man.

. . . I prayed till my mind became so full that, before I was aware of it, I was on my feet and tripping up the ascent toward the road. The question of my being converted, had not so much as arisen to my thought; but as I went up, brushing through the leaves and bushes, I recollect saying with great emphasis, "If I am ever converted, I will preach the Gospel."

I soon reached the road that led to the village, and began to reflect upon what had passed; and I found that my mind had become most wonderfully quiet and peaceful. . . .

I walked quietly toward the village; and so perfectly quiet was my mind that it seemed as if all nature listened. It was on the 10th of October, and a very pleasant day. I had gone into the woods immediately after an early breakfast; and when I returned to the village I found it was dinner time. Yet I had been wholly unconscious of the time that had passed; it appeared to me that I had been gone from the village but a short time.

But how was I to account for the quiet of my mind? I tried to recall my convictions, to get back again the load of sin under which I had been laboring. But all sense of sin, all consciousness of present sin or guilt, had departed from me. I said to myself, "What is this, that I cannot arouse any sense of guilt in my soul, as great a sinner as I am?" I tried in vain to make myself anxious about my present state. I was so quiet and peaceful that I tried to feel concerned about that, lest it should be a result of my having grieved the Spirit away. But take any view of it I would, I could not be anxious at all about my soul, and about my spiritual state. The repose of my mind was unspeakably great. I never can describe it in words. The thought of God was sweet to my mind, and the most profound spiritual tranquillity had taken full possession of me.[3]

Charles Grandison Finney found God! Or, as he would have wanted it said, God found Finney.

Still, Finney was not quite ready for the mighty revival ministry he was to exercise; he needed a gracious infilling of the Holy Spirit's power. Now note again, as in the case of Roberts and Wesley, Finney was truly converted and thus possessed the Holy Spirit. Really, one never receives *in principle* anything one did not receive at the moment of conversion. That is the fundamental foundation of *all* spiritual experience. Yet the young, newly converted lawyer stood in need of *power for service*. Finney must be filled with "revival" if he were to bring it to others.

In Finney's experience, there was hardly any time span between his conversion and God's challenge for revival ministry by a mighty filling of the Holy Spirit. Of course, there need not be any delay. Thus, on the evening of the same day that Finney was transformed from a critical doubter to a consecrated disciple of Jesus Christ, God did a marvelous work in granting him power for service. The experience is such that it too must be related from his own pen. Finney's narrative continues:

> . . . I then went to the office, and found that Squire W_____ had gone to dinner. I took down my bass-viol, and, as I was accustomed to do, began to play and sing some pieces of sacred music. But as soon as I began to sing those sacred words, I began to weep. It seemed as if my heart was all liquid; and my feelings were in such a state that I could not hear my own voice in singing without causing my sensibility to overflow. I wondered at this, and tried to suppress my tears, but could not. After trying in vain to suppress my tears, I put up my instrument and stopped singing. . . .
>
> By evening we got the books and furniture adjusted; and I made up, in an open fire-place, a good fire, hoping to spend the evening alone. Just at dark Squire W_____, seeing that everything was adjusted, bade me good-night and went to his home. I had accompanied him to the door; and as I closed the door and turned around, my heart seemed to be liquid within me. All my feelings seemed to rise and flow out; and the utterance of my heart was, "I want to pour my whole soul out to God." The rising

of my soul was so great that I rushed into the room back of the front office, to pray.

There was no fire, and no light, in the room; nevertheless it appeared to me as if it were perfectly light. As I went in and shut the door after me, it seemed as if I met the Lord Jesus Christ face to face. It did not occur to me then, nor did it for some time afterward, that it was wholly a mental state. On the contrary it seemed to me that I saw him as I would see any other man. He said nothing, but looked at me in such a manner as to break me right down at his feet. I have always since regarded this as a most remarkable state of mind; for it seemed to me a reality, that he stood before me, and I fell down at his feet and poured out my soul to him. I wept aloud like a child, and made such confessions as I could with my choked utterance. It seemed to me that I bathed his feet with my tears. . . .

I must have continued in this state for a good while; but my mind was too much absorbed with the interview to recollect anything that I said. But I know, as soon as my mind became calm enough to break off from the interview, I returned to the front office, and found that the fire that I had made of large wood was nearly burned out. But as I turned and was about to take a seat by the fire, I received a mighty baptism of the Holy Ghost. Without any expectation of it, without ever having the thought in my mind that there was any such thing for me, without any recollection that I had ever heard the thing mentioned by any person in the world, the Holy Spirit descended upon me in a manner that seemed to go through me, body and soul. . . . Indeed it seemed to come in waves and waves of liquid love; for I could not express it in any other way. It seemed like the very breath of God. I can recollect distinctly that it seemed to fan me, like immense wings.

No words can express the wonderful love that was shed abroad in my heart. I wept aloud with joy and love. . . . These waves came over me, and over me, one after the other, until I recollect I cried out, "I shall die if these waves continue to pass over me." I said, "Lord, I cannot bear any more;" yet I had no fear of death.

How long I continued in this state, with this baptism continuing to roll over me and go through me, I do not know. But I know it was late in the evening when a member of my choir—for I was the leader of the choir—came into the office to see me. He was a member of the church. He found me in this state of loud weeping, and said to me, "Mr. Finney, what ails you?" I could make him no answer for some time. He then said, "Are you in pain?" I gathered myself up as best I could, and replied, "No, but so happy that I cannot live."

. . . . . . . . . . . . . . . . . . . . . . . . . . . . . . . . . . . . . . . . . . . . . . . . . . . . . . .

When I awoke in the morning the sun had risen, and was pouring a clear light into my room. Words cannot express the impression that this sunlight made upon me. Instantly the baptism that I had received the night before, returned upon me in the same manner. I arose upon my knees in the bed and wept aloud with joy, and remained for some time too much over-whelmed with the baptism of the Spirit to do anything but pour out my soul to God. It seemed as if this morning's baptism was accompanied with a gentle reproof, and the Spirit seemed to say to me, "Will you doubt?" "Will you doubt?" I cried, "No! I will not doubt; I cannot doubt." He then cleared the subject up so much to my mind that it was in fact impossible for me to doubt that the Spirit of God had taken possession of my soul.[4]

From that experience, young Finney went out to preach with a power rarely encountered. Revival broke out everywhere he ministered. All the way from little Evans Mills, New York, to Henry Ward Beecher's great church in Boston, Massachusetts, awakenings erupted like exploding volcanoes. Whole towns were converted. Never has America produced a more powerful preacher. Finney will always stand as the archetype of a revivalist. God did something through his revival services that is seldom seen.

## The Prime Point Again

That October 10, 1821, was a fantastic day for Charles G. Finney. Through it the prime point is again projected and stands out in bold relief; God revives churches and nations through revived people. *It starts with those whom God can fully possess.*

Of course, there are many vitally important implications of

the truth concerning the Holy Spirit's work that must be understood from the Bible. These issues will be taken up in detail in the chapter on the Spirit-filled life. But let it be understood and stressed at this point that the Spirit of God deeply desires to touch *all* our lives, revive us *all*, fit *everyone* of us for effective service for our Lord Jesus Christ. That is really the sum and substance of what took place in the deep experiences of Evan Roberts, John Wesley, and Charles Finney. The emotions and dramatic circumstances were quite secondary. They were no more than filled, fitted, and revived for service.

But, we are prone to retort, all of that is history. It is surely inspiring, but does God really want to do that kind of thing for us, today? Can such an experience truly be ours? We are just ordinary Christians, we say. The answer is *Yes!* God does want to do a deep reviving work in us all. Granted, the circumstances, emotions, and other secondary aspects will probably be entirely different for us than for those of history. This has been stressed several times. *But the principle is the same.* We, as they of the past, need God's reviving power if our Christian experience is to be rich, meaningful, and useful to others. If a general awakening is to dawn, we must be the first to feel its rays. If a great revival is to break, we are to be revived first. But is a revival coming? Can we expect a great awakening in our day? And if so, does God want to use us? These are important questions.

What about the contemporary moment? Can the Holy Spirit fall once more upon our churches, our country, our complete cosmos? Is there any hope for us in our time?

There are those in the contemporary Christian drama who believe a revival is in the wings. I join them, for there are many important indicators that such a movement is just waiting for that divine cue to burst on the scene of the twentieth century stage. It seems that God is trying to say today what he said to Israel long ago: "Comfort, comfort my people, says your God./

Speak tenderly to Jerusalem,/and cry to her/that her warfare is ended,/that her iniquity is pardoned" (Isa. 40:1-2). The day is at hand.

## Revival Signs

When will the longed for revival come? James Burns describes several "straws in the wind pointing to a coming moving of God." For example, an awakening normally meshes in synchronization with national events. When social, political, and economic crises develop, revival is often God's solution. As one looks at the sociological revolution endured for the last two decades, the present apathy notwithstanding, all hearts should resound in an anticipatory cry for revival.

Another "straw" indicating the coming awakening is the feeling of helplessness in the church to cope with its pressing problems. Thankfully, there are some bright spots, yet many congregations are in despair. But if this despair can deepen into burden, there is real hope. If despair can drive the church to sincere, sacrificial prayer, God can act.

Finally, Burns holds that when there is concern for world missions and evangelism, an awakening may be imminent. It has been many years since segments of the church have shown such enthusiasm as they now do for the evangelization of our world. All these factors must surely mean something. Could it be that an awakening is already on the way?[5]

No one has grasped these principles more clearly than Charles G. Finney. He is most helpful because he hammered out his ideas in the white-hot fervor of the spiritual awakening that erupted in the context of his ministry.

## Finney's Principles

Finney finds the prophet Habakkuk praying the proper prayer: "O Lord, revive thy work in the midst of the years, in

the midst of the years make known; in wrath remember mercy"
(Hab. 3:2*b*). The preacher anticipated anguish; Judah's defeat
and captivity were at hand. So the prophet prayed, "O Lord,
revive thy work." It is as if he said, "O Lord, grant that thy
judgments may not make Israel desolate. In the midst of these
awful years, let the judgments of God be made the means of
reviving religion among us. In wrath remember mercy."

This sets the stage for the drama of revival. An awakening
can be anticipated when society degenerates to its lowest level,
just when it seems there could never be a move of God. When
disobedience, immorality, secularism, and godlessness prevail,
the situation is ripe for revival. This sounds much like our
current situation.

Further, an awakening is essential when brotherly love
wanes. Where is the deep fellowship that should prevail among
the whole of God's people? There are small fellowship groups,
but where is the spirit of *agape*, self-giving love? Finney states,
"When there are dissensions, and jealousies, and evil speak-
ings . . . then there is great need of a revival."[6] This, too, speaks
to the contemporary scene.

When worldliness grips the church, a revival is desperately
needed. In times past, Christians have been sensitive about the
invasion of worldly ways, ambitions, pleasures, and carnal
values into their lives. Now it seems we have not only let down
the barriers but have become blasé about it. We appear to be
proud of our worldly attitudes and value systems and look with
an air of superiority at the old morality and puritanical principles. I wonder how God feels about that.

Finney further states that open sin in the church demonstrates the need of new life. Church discipline, even if not well
handled in the past, is now all but forgotten. Now a church
member can deal deceitfully in business, curse, and tell off-
color stories with impunity. About all that is ever done about it

is to raise a few eyebrows. No wonder the world looks at the church with disdain, if not disgust.

Finally, when the lost are unconcerned, even when they hear the gospel, an awakening is sorely needed. In America at least, the gospel has all but saturated the nation. Radio, television, the printed page, all the media are deluged with gospel messages. Yet millions plunge on unheeding. Why? We need the presence of God in quickening power to make the gospel alive. Finney laid out these principles many years ago, yet their relevance is obvious.

Any insightful observer can see that the current scene is set for the drama of a great awakening. I am convinced a new, refreshing, spiritual revival is about to break. Moreover, it seems obvious that this kind of movement is our only hope, personally, in our churches, and in our world. Surely, we are all aware of the need of a true touch from God to awaken and deepen us all. But the day is at hand when God will "bend" his children and subsequently see us "filled with all the fulness of God" (Eph. 3:19). Our Lord is going to revive his work and that right soon.

All of that now leads to the basic question we have already faced: What about us "ordinary" Christians in it all? Few of us have had the traumatic spiritual upheavals of a Roberts, Wesley, or Finney. Will God use us? Again say, Certainly! The Spirit of God hovers over all his people seeking the ones he can "bend" and fill. True, God may never give us a great emotional upheaval; he may come to us as a "still small voice" (1 Kings 19:12). He often has in the past. But the promise is: God will surely address us, supply our needs, and fill to overflowing our empty lives *if* we will but permit him to do so. If we are open to his challenge, he will meet us and use us. Granted, our contribution to Christ's service and kingdom may not be on a grand scale as the world counts grandness, but any way in which God chooses to use us is grand. It may not make the newspapers on earth, but it will make headlines in heaven.

Then it must not be forgotten on the other hand that Roberts, Wesley, Finney, and many others never conceived in their wildest dreams the plans God had for their rather average lives, average, that is, *before* they were revived. They too saw themselves as quite "ordinary." But God obviously used them greatly. It may be that God will use us far more significantly than we ever thought possible. We must let God be God and use us and do with us as He sees fit, quietly or dramatically. I suppose for many of us it will be rather quietly, but one thing is certain, if any reviving—small or great—comes to our world today, God must have a revived people. This is why the Spirit of God would revive all of his people. This is why the Holy Spirit would revive you. It must begin somewhere.

## The Basic Question

Therefore, the sincere believer who wants God's best is directly faced with the basic question: How is one revived? How does a Christian actually enter into that sort of spiritual power life-style? If these questions are asked from the perspective of a genuine thirst for God's touch, then the Holy Spirit has something to quench that thirst in the truth of his Word. The Bible holds the clue, as always. The quest for a revived life emerges in the context of a biblical understanding of basic Christian experiences. Therefore, to this scriptural quest we turn.

Moses my servant is dead; now therefore arise, go over this Jordan, you and all this people, into the land which I am giving to them, to the people of Israel. Every place that the sole of your foot will tread upon I have given to you, as I promised to Moses. . . . Be strong and of good courage; for you shall cause this people to inherit the land which I swore to their fathers to give them. (Joshua 1:2,3,6)

# 2
# The Revived Life Is
# an Abandoned Life

"God broke my heart!" That is how the pastor described the beginning of a modern-day church reviving. The story that emerged out of the pastor's statement is fascinating.

Pastor Elvis Marcum graduated from seminary and settled in a small, struggling work in New Albany, Indiana, just across the river from Louisville, Kentucky, where he had attended Southern Baptists' oldest theological school. The Graceland Baptist Church was a difficult pastorate from the outset. The people had even seriously considered disbanding before Marcum came. Nothing seemed to go well. For example, only fourteen people came to their first evangelistic service during Marcum's early ministry. The disappointing response was indicative of the entire situation. Pastor Marcum's days were seemingly packed full of struggle and discouragement. There was one bright spot shining through these dismal days, however. A dear elderly lady, Miss Clara Myers, was a true prayer

warrior. The young pastor often visited her in his discouragement. This lovely lady would always say, "Brother Marcum, do
not be depressed. *It will be better.*" She spoke these words with
such conviction that it was evident she was prevailing with
God. These visits kept the pastor pressing on.

The testing times were many. "Revivals," in the sense of local
evangelistic crusades, simply did not work. They were abandoned. The church turned to various social ministries and had
a measure of blessing. Still, the overall impact of the Graceland
Baptist Church in the New Albany community left much to be
desired, even though a reasonably good growth pattern began
to evolve.

This style of church life continued for almost a decade. Then
the pastor was introduced to the historical phenomenon of
great awakenings—"revival" in the classical understanding of
the word. He was enthralled and taken up with what God does
when the Holy Spirit falls in genuine reviving power. He began
preaching, teaching, and instructing his people in the principles of awakenings. Above all, he began earnestly interceding
for such a move of God upon his church. He became absolutely
convinced this was God's will for Graceland. They must experience *real* revival.

In September, 1977, Marcum became desperate. He saw no
deep movement of the Spirit, despite all his efforts to promote
an awakening. In the midst of that depression, *God broke him,*
really broke him, and showed him what he actually was in the
sight of a holy, sovereign God. His heart was crushed with
conviction. It took him days, he readily admitted, to put
everything right with God and make restitution to those he had
wronged. In his own words, that was the beginning of revival.
That is always the beginning, as we have amply seen. Historically or contemporarily, God has to get us yielded to his
sovereign will before he can do great things for us and through

us. Graceland was now getting ready for a touch from God; a man had been "broken."

The church moved into a twenty-four-hour prayer ministry. Things began to look up. Of course, Miss Myers continued to prevail with God. Then in March, 1979, Marcum suffered a massive heart attack. He thought it was all over. His health was shattered. The only course seemed to be resignation and retirement. At that point he was deeply impressed he should not retire because he would be restored. God did touch him. Competent medical evaluation has demonstrated he is now a well man.

Now Marcum felt he had a word from the Lord; revival would soon come to Graceland. He held this up to the people. In faith, the church claimed the promise of 2 Chronicles 7:14: "If my people who are called by my name humble themselves, and pray and seek my face, and turn from their wicked ways, then I will hear from heaven, and will forgive their sin and heal their land." The pastor and his praying people stormed heaven's gates as never before.

Marcum continued to lead the congregation into the truths of revival as much as they were able to bear it. Many grew to the point of faith where they were able to take God at his bare Word and claim in full assurance the promise of 2 Chronicles 7:14.

Miss Clara had been praying in that spirit for years. She kept telling Pastor Marcum, "There is a better day coming." Then in 1979 she died. She never saw the awakening she had so sacrificially and fervently prayed for—at least she did not see it from this world's vantage point.

The Graceland faithful kept interceding. Still, no real evidence of revival was forthcoming. The praying people grew more and more desperate in their pleading with God for an awakening.

On Saturday, May 17, 1980, the break began to come. That

night Pastor Marcum was so burdened he went to the church building at midnight and fell before God on a kneeling rail they had constructed in the auditorium. He felt he must see holy living in the church's leadership. He was convinced they must deal with this issue. Such was his overwhelming burden in prayer.

The prayer group took up the theme in their intercession. The next Sunday, Marcum laid it out to the church and stressed the need of personal holiness.

Right at that moment, Jim Hylton, pastor of the Lake Country Baptist Church in Fort Worth, Texas, came to Graceland to conduct a four-day Bible conference. A spirit of deep, profound conviction was manifest at the very outset of the meeting—and it was not even billed as a "revival." But terminology does not hinder God; the Holy Spirit began to move in great power. In a stroke, so it seemed, the whole situation was transformed. Hylton himself admitted that he too was radically changed by it all; he had expected nothing like this. God had come at last.

The long-prayed-for awakening dawned. From the first service, the altars filled, the transformation of lives abounded, and many were converted—including several church members. Confession and deliverance from sin and Satan's power were manifest. There were even a few medically authenticated marvelous physical healings. Jim Hylton preached with overwhelming power.

In all the varied manifestations of the movement there persisted a beautiful biblical balance. The thrust never degenerated into any emotional excess or doctrinal error. The Holy Spirit made the Book of Mark particularly alive to the pastor and people. That kept them on an even keel. God was in obvious control.

Great multitudes did not come to the meetings at first. It was just a profound revival of the church itself. But as the word began to spread, people started arriving from all over the county to share in the blessings.

God's people at Graceland continued to get thoroughly right with God and others by confession and restitution. The daily services went on for three months. Hylton's four-day Bible conference got rather elongated, to say the least. Financial needs were high due to the expense of holding so many meetings. But the faithful got under the burden and responded sacrificially. One dedicated lady even gave her rings to help carry on the work. She had no cash, but she had a few jewels. These she gladly gave. The people felt deeply and responded accordingly.

About this time a dedicated dentist, Dr. Findley Baird of Louisville, came to the pastor. He told Marcum he felt led of God to cancel all his meetings—he is a lay speaker sought after all around the world. He wanted to join the effort and train lay people to share their faith. This he did, at no small sacrifice. The work almost immediately deepened. There are now two hundred lay persons engaged in personal witnessing. Moreover, as new converts come into the church, they are immediately taught and sent out as witnesses. The social ministry of the church continues at a great pace as well. Hence the work keeps multiplying. When asked why he thought the revival had come to Graceland, Dr. Baird said, "The pastor was *open to all God said.*" And that is the key—God got his instrument.

Graceland Baptist Church is having its day of glory. But be clear; all that the awakening aroused was actualized when the Holy Spirit broke hearts and stirred up a heavenly hunger for holiness. God's people *must* move into the fullness of holy, committed, surrendered fellowship with Jesus Christ if they are to experience a genuine revived life. And that is usually a long—often lonely—journey. The road is filled with many dangerous curves and perilous pitfalls. But that route is also filled with excitement, joy, and victories. The rewards are well worth the venture.

## The Christian Journey

In the New Testament, the Christian experience of traveling toward holiness is sometimes illustrated by comparing it with the journey of Israel from Egypt to the Promised Land. This approach is taken, for example, in Hebrews, chapters 3–5. The Scriptures tell us that Israel—God's people of old—traveled a long, laborious route before finding fullness in Canaan; the land that "flowed with milk and honey." It can be no different for contemporary Christians. Therefore, let's take the trip with them. It is unfolded in the Old Testament in three significant stages. Israel's first move was:

### The Exodus from Egypt

A survey of Old Testament history reveals that the Hebrews became a great nation in the land of the Pharaohs. They had entered as a small, single family many years prior. After four centuries they had multiplied by God's blessings into a nation of hundreds of thousands. In the latter part of their Egyptian sojourn a pharaoh arose who "knew not Joseph" (Ex. 1:8, KJV)—and trouble, real trouble, tumbled in on them.

Out of jealousy, greed, and downright fear, the Egyptians thrust the Jews under the heel of oppression and reduced them to abject slavery. Life became bitter. All day long they were forced to grovel under the whip of their sadistic taskmasters. No freedom. No status. No self-esteem. Nothing to call their own, not even their own lives. What a pitiful plight! That's slavery.

Few of us know anything in any real way about that sort of

life-style. But we can imagine. Heartache, loneliness, isolation, depression, *misery!* There is no joy, meaning, purpose, or reality in slave-like bondage.

Finally, for many of the Hebrew slaves, Egypt became their burial ground. They simply died because of it all. To live out one's life as a miserable slave is tragic! To die as one is unthinkable.

That is the story of the Jews in Egypt.

It should be crystal clear why the Egyptian bondage is so often likened to a life without God. The parallel is arresting. The experience of the Hebrews pictures perfectly any person who does not know our Lord Jesus Christ.

First, without Christ one is a slave. Of course, one may well think he is free to do as he pleases. Yet nothing could be further from the truth. Bound to base appetites; shackled to Satan; wound up in this world; fettered to fear and frustrations: that is one's *true* condition apart from God's great redemption through his Son. This is why our Lord Jesus Christ said, "So if the Son sets you free, you will be free indeed" (John 8:36, NIV).

Furthermore, a life lived apart from Jesus Christ is, in the final analysis, one of privation, heartache, depression, and gloom. Granted, there are the "pleasures of sin for a season" (Heb. 11:25, KJV). The world and all its glitter, the flesh and its lust have their momentary thrill. It is a "blast while it lasts," but that is the sting; it only lasts "for a season." With a life unyielded to God, there is an inevitable backwash of depressing guilt and gloom that tarnishes every joy and finally destroys meaning, purpose, and reality in life. Slaves to self are simply never satisfied.

Finally, slaves die. It is true, even in our modern, highly educated, technological, secular society; the "wages of sin is death" (Rom. 6:23, KJV). "The soul that sins shall die" (Ezek. 18:20). There is no life apart from Jesus Christ.

The Israelites desperately needed to be delivered from their Egyptian bondage. If we are without the liberating, redeeming, life-giving power of Jesus Christ in our lives, we stand in far greater need of God's releasing grace. I am aware that most of the readers of these words have experienced "redemption from Egypt." But if you have not, or are not certain, cry to God for deliverance as did Israel of old. Trust Christ as Lord and Savior and *come out of Egypt!*

That is what the Hebrews did—they cried to God for deliverance. And God heard their anguished plea. He always does. Moses, the deliverer, was sent.

The Exodus account laid out so dramatically in the second book of the Bible is thrilling! God bared his powerful arm and proved himself "mighty to save" (Isa. 63:1). In the strong name of their God, the Hebrews strode out triumphantly as a redeemed people—redeemed from slavery, misery, and death. "Free at last, free at last," hallelujah, "free at last"!

God led his people in a marvelous way. The Red Sea parted; the covenant of the Law was given; and by a pillar of cloud in the day and a pillar of fire in the night, they were directed to the little town of Kadesh-barnea that bordered Canaan on the south. Before them stretched out a beautiful country that flowed with milk and honey, that lovely land which they had not seen for over four hundred years. "Go in and possess it," God said. "I gave it to your forefathers; it is yours for the taking." What a day of victory for the Jewish people! *But then tragedy struck.*

Like the dark, ominous clouds that roll in from the Mediterranean to blot out the warm Palestinian sun, dark clouds of doubt and confusion rolled over Israel as they camped at Kadesh-barnea. The lightning of rebellion soon flashed, and they cried out in fear to Moses, We will "go back to Egypt." And the die was cast. They were doomed to a life of wandering.

## Wandering in the Wilderness

Forty years! Forty, long, depressing, trying, years! Wandering about in that dry, barren, miserable Sinai Desert, never inheriting their inheritance, never possessing their possessions, Israel became the wilderness-wandering people of God. And they had been redeemed from Egypt. Think of it. The redeemed of the Lord doomed to the desert. What a tragedy, we say. Correct! The Kadesh-barnea incident was an unparalleled blunder. Yet as the "new Israel," God's contemporary redeemed people, we often repeat the same tragic error. Is it really uncommon when some new challenge or circumstance crosses our path to begin to see the dark clouds of doubt and fear creep across our lives, blotting out the sunshine of God's promise of victory? Then the lightning flash of rebellion throws its jagged prong over our path and we take the first step in its direction, only to realize that it finally leads away from God. The die is cast; into a barren, desertlike experience of God we grope and wander around, never inheriting our inheritance or possessing our possessions. Thus we become "wilderness-wandering Christians."

As spiritual Egypt is characteristic of those who do not know Jesus Christ, so is spiritual Sinai of those who have not inherited all the *fullness* of Christ. What is it like to wander about as a barren Christian?

*Spiritual Warfare*—First, wilderness-wandering Christians find themselves locked in mortal conflict with themselves, fighting, struggling, battling. The result is constant inner conflict. Of course, it is easy to retort: That's the way the Christian life is intended to be. Do we not sing "Onward, Christian soldiers,/Marching as to war?" (Sabine Baring-Gould, "Onward, Christian Soldiers"). The Bible even says "the desires of the flesh are against the Spirit, and the desires of the Spirit are against the flesh" (Gal. 5:17). True, but when we war in the wilderness we find ourselves constantly, repeatedly defeated. And that robs one of all Christian joy and peace in spiritual experience.

Strange as it may seem, even the apostle Paul endured that sort of depressing struggle at one stage in his spiritual sojourn. He bares his heart and in an anguished admission states:

> I do not understand my own actions. For I do not do what I want, but I do the very thing I hate. . . . For I know that nothing good dwells within me, that is, in my flesh. I can will what is right, but I cannot do it. For I do not do the good I want, but the evil I do not want is what I do. . . . Wretched man that I am! Who will deliver me from this body of death? (Rom. 7:15,18-19,24).

Some Bible scholars continually quibble over whether this confession was "pre" or "post" Paul's experience of redemption in Christ, that is, whether the apostle was speaking from "Egypt" or "the wilderness." But that is not the prime point, at least experientially. It really makes no difference whether he is speaking as a Christian or not. All who are not in "Canaan" are going to endure something very much like that in their spiritual journeys.

What is Paul actually attempting to relate? Let us assume he is speaking as a believer. He seems to be saying something like this: "I am a believer in Jesus Christ. This implies several very important facts. To begin with, the Holy Spirit lives in my life. He inspires me to do many good things. Moreover, I love the Lord. He has saved me. I am out of 'Egypt.' Therefore, I want to do those good deeds. There is 'good that I would' do."

Of course, the list of these "good things" is all but endless. Merely to recount them demands too many pages for this volume. Just a few to illustrate the point will have to suffice— though with these ideas one can easily identify the problem.

Bible study is an excellent example. How often as Christians we determine to delve into the Word of God far more profoundly than in the past. God's Spirit challenges us that the few snatches of Scripture we often try to sustain our souls upon are simply insufficient for genuine Christian growth. Conviction grips us. So we promise ourselves, perhaps even God, that we will begin to dig deep and mine the rich treasures of the Bible.

The corollary to Bible study, prayer, is another case in point. All spiritually-minded believers understand the centrality and absolute necessity of prayer for a healthy experience in Jesus Christ. All are well aware that the great victories in the kingdom of God are not won by human, feverish activity. Rather, they are accomplished in the prayer closets. The annals of God's history are filled with such accounts.

Several years ago a young minister, after graduating from the seminary, traveled to the west coast of America and boarded a ship bound for India. He had dedicated his life to the mission field. When he excitedly entered his stateroom, a telegram awaited him. Thinking it a bon voyage message he eagerly opened it to find it was sent by an old pastor and friend. The communication simply asked, "John, are you filled with the Holy Spirit?"

Young missionary John Hyde was rather taken back and became indignant. *Imagine*, he thought, *asking a question like that. Here I am, dedicated to the mission field. I'm making a great sacrifice. What a question to ask!* He crumpled up the telegram, flung it on the floor, and stamped out to the deck.

The Lord's arrow had penetrated Hyde's proud young heart deeply, however. There was no extracting the barb. He paced the deck, paced the deck, paced the deck. Finally, the Holy Spirit utterly broke his proud servant, and John absolutely abandoned his life to God and sought the fullness of the Holy Spirit for his missionary service.

The amazing ministry that emerged after the crisis was unique. The Holy Spirit molded John Hyde into a profound prayer warrior. The subcontinent of India had never seen a missionary quite like this young man. His prayer life deepened and expanded until he was actually praying four hours a day. It is not incidental that God was at the same time permitting him to win four Indians to Christ every day.

John grew quite ill. He was given a thorough medical examination. When the tests were returned and the missionary called in, the doctor exclaimed, "John, what have you been doing to yourself? What stress are you subjecting yourself to? Your physical heart has moved some distance in your chest cavity through stress and strain. What in the world are you doing?" When he died some years later, India as a nation mourned that devoted missionary. The eulogies that were lovingly lifted up to his memory were all addressed to the name by which all India knew him: not John Hyde, his real name, but *Praying* Hyde, the name they loved.

When we encounter stories like that, our hearts convict us of our prayerlessness. We determine to pray more, and we mean it. It is a "good" we would do.

The list of the "good" goes on growing: witnessing to the lost, faithful service to the church, and so on. We do want to be "good" people.

But when the crunch comes, that is, when it comes to the actual *doing* of all those "good things" with disciplined consistency, the problems begin. Determine as we will, vow as we might, it seems we never truly rise to our high resolves. Down in defeat we are constantly dragged, not doing the very thing we wish. Thus we find ourselves forced to confess with Paul, "the good that I would I do not" (KJV).

Moreover, there is another side to the coin—a negative side. Paul expressed it this way: "the evil which I would not, that I do" (KJV). Even as the Holy Spirit lives within and inspires "the good," he also puts some prohibitions before the people of God. Even though Christianity is essentially positive, there are some "thou shalt nots" for the true believer. That list is lengthy also: prejudice, grumbling, evil desires, entertaining lustful thoughts, unkind words, gossip, and the like.

We do not desire to harbor such sins; after all, Christ has saved us. Yet they tend to creep into our experience. So we ask God to forgive us and determine we will never permit such things in our lives again. But after the moment of challenge and conviction is passed, circumstances set themselves up just right—the adversary knows how to arrange that—and out from Satan's bow flies a fiery arrow of temptation, strikes our spiritual Achilles' heel, and headlong we fall into the very sin we said we would forsake. Honesty thus compels us to make the acknowledgment with Paul, "The evil which I would not, that I do."

Granted, there are some victories for any Christian. Israel defeated the Amalekites in the wilderness (Ex. 17:8-16). But still we seem to fall so miserably short of our goal of devoted Christlike living. Defeat more than victory characterizes our wilderness-wandering lives.

So we battle and strive only to be repeatedly defeated until we are all but reduced to despair, ready to throw up our hands and plaintively cry with Paul, "O wretched man that I am! who shall deliver me from the body of this death?" (Rom. 7:24).

Do you ever feel like that—at least to some extent? The problem is you may be wandering in the spiritual wilderness. God has something far better for his people.

✓ *Protracted Infancy*—The wilderness is a wasteland of warfare. It is also a place of protracted infancy regarding spiritual growth. When I was a good bit younger, I had a job working as a delivery man for a small, local grocery store. Those were the days when you could telephone an order to your favorite store and the groceries would be brought to your home—some time ago to be sure!

Every Saturday, my responsibility was to deliver an order of groceries to a certain home. I always approached that particular place with a bit of dread. It never failed to be something of a wrench to walk into the home. The family was not unkind; on the contrary, they were lovely folks. But on entering the kitchen and placing the order of groceries on the table, my eyes were irresistibly drawn to the next room. There on a daybed lay their son. Judging by the age of the parents, the boy must have been in his twenties. Yet he had never matured mentally or physically from infancy. There he was, warped, twisted, in such a sad state. A tragedy to these dear people? Of course—perhaps you know something of that sadness yourself.

Another great tragedy is packed with pathos and pity. God has thousands, even millions, of children just like that son. That is why the writer of Hebrews exclaimed, "For though by this time you ought to be teachers, you need some one to teach you again the first principles of God's word" (Heb. 5:12). In other words, the writer is saying, "As long as you have been Christians, you should by this time be strong, growing, healthy, spiritual teachers, and you are still babes in Christ." What a pity—still babes!

Of course, babies are sweet and lovable. But we must honestly grant they are also a bundle of self, and if they do not get their own way they can raise a ruckus. It reminds one of the Israelites in the Sinai Desert. You can almost hear their incessant complaint, "Moses, Moses, Moses, all you have given us to eat is manna, manna, manna."

Perhaps we should not be too critical of that complaining crowd. Their unhappiness over the menu is somewhat understandable. Think of it: manna for breakfast, manna for lunch, manna for the evening meal, manna for the midnight snack! Day after day, month after month, for forty long, depressing years it was only manna for every meal. I venture to say they baked it, boiled it, stewed it, scalloped it, fried it, did everything to it, but it always came out *manna*. Finally, the Israelites threw up their hands and cried, "Our souls loathe this food." Now those Hebrews should not have complained and carried on as they did. Manna was God's provision. Yet it was not the Lord's *perfect* will. Over in Canaan was a land that flowed with milk and honey. They had forfeited that at Kadesh-barnea, and they were subsisting on manna of *their own choice*.

Oh, to be any place but in the wilderness! How depressing. No fruit bearing, constant defeat, protracted infancy, and on and on. Anything must be better than a wilderness-wandering Christian experience. That is surely not revival living. Thus we are led to ask: "What is it like over in Canaan?"

## The Promised Land

To summarize at the outset, spiritual Canaan is the antithesis—the exact opposite—of all one experiences in the wilderness.

First, it is a life of growth in the grace and knowledge of our Lord Jesus Christ (2 Pet. 3:18). As a very young Christian—I had only been saved a matter of months—I found myself in the military, stationed in southern Florida. I soon learned in that situation that if I were to survive spiritually, I would have to maintain a disciplined devotional life. I also soon learned that a military barracks is hardly conducive to Scripture reading and prayer. What goes on in a barracks rarely lifts one heavenward. Our chaplain was sensitive to this problem, so a small room was set aside at the base chapel for those who wished a "quiet time" with the Lord.

One Saturday night I walked down to the chapel to spend a few moments with the Lord. I looked forward to a happy time in fellowship with my newfound Savior. Arriving at the chapel and entering the vestibule, I heard someone inside preaching. I thought I would slip in and enjoy the sermon. To my surprise, the building was empty, except for one, lone preacher, and he was not a chaplain. The man in the pulpit was a "GI" preaching to empty pews.

When the young preacher saw me, he stopped, and we fell into conversation. Almost immediately, that young man began to amaze me. He shared scriptural truths I had never encountered; his prayer life was alive and vibrant; he had won several of his barrack mates to Christ. God had called him to the ministry. He was addressing the empty pews because a small church off the military base had asked him to preach, and he was practicing his sermon.

To be quite frank, I became a little spiritually envious. I thought to myself, *I wonder if I will ever grow to the depth of spiritual maturity of this young Christian.* But then, I was a Christian of only a few months—you can't expect too much of yourself in so short a time.

At that moment, the young preacher all but shocked me. He told me he, too, had been saved only a mere matter of months. Although I knew he had a very fine Christian background to draw upon after his conversion, I still could not understand how one could grow so rapidly in the Spirit in so short a time. I did not quite grasp it all then, but I do now. That young man had crossed the river Jordan from the wilderness and was living out his spiritual experience in Canaan. For over on the other side of the river, one grows by proverbial leaps and bounds. Fruit bearing just naturally occurs. God can do more for and through his children in five months if they are in the "Promised Land" than in five years if they persist in wilderness wandering. Revived Christians grow.

## Christian Victory

Perhaps the Canaan-dwelling Christian life can all be summed up in that word which should always characterize God's people: VICTORY. Paul's triumphant claim was, "We are more than conquerors through him who loved us" (Rom. 8:37). Paul did not remain in a depressing Romans 7 experience; he moved into the victorious life-style presented in Romans 8. Over there, everything is radically different. Victory attends the Canaan-dwelling Christian.

The curtain drops on our journeying drama as I relate the most profound story of Christian victory I have ever heard. When I was a seminary student I asked the wife of one of our international students to come and share her testimony to my small student pastorate. The account unfolded as follows:

In the early days of World War II, before America was embroiled in the Pacific hostilities, Ahn Kim was a woman of devout prayer and Bible study in her native Korea. She had memorized many lengthy passages and entire chapters of the Bible. Hours were spent before God in earnest intercession. As she prayed one day, she felt impressed to travel to Tokyo and proclaim to the warlords of Japan that unless they repented and turned to Jesus Christ the judgment of God would come upon their nation.

That, of course, was unthinkable, especially in the Far East under wartime circumstances. But she could not escape the impression. She struggled for days to know God's will. Finally, convinced of her conviction, she purchased a one-way ticket to Tokyo.

God marvelously opened doors, and she soon found herself in one of the small spectators' alcoves that overlooked the Japanese Diet (Congress) in wartime session. There were assembled the nation's significant leaders.

A lull crept into the proceedings, and Ahn jumped to her feet and cried out, "Leaders of Japan." A hush settled over the scene, and every eye riveted on her.

She had her declaration written on a little scroll. Unrolling the document, she read out judgment. "Unless you repent and turn to Jesus Christ, God will judge you," she warned. They sat there spellbound—nothing like that had ever happened before. After finishing her speech, she rolled up the scroll, threw it down in their midst, and turned to walk away. When the assembly recovered from their stunned amazement, she was taken prisoner. Strangely, she was not summarily executed as she had expected—hence the one-way ticket. Even more unusual, perhaps, she was sent back to Korea and thrown in prison. But it was there that her story of victory in Christ truly begins.

Back in her native country, she was forced into a cell not more than ten by twenty-five feet. In that cell there were crammed twenty other prisoners. Her description of the filth and stench of that unbelievably crowded cell with no sanitation was almost sickening. She suffered so from malnutrition that she lost her hair and went blind. As the guards once a day brought in their small ration of rice, she said it seemed that some great hand would reach up and snatch it into her emaciated frame before she could even taste it. She deteriorated into one of those bloat-bellied, living skeletons we have all seen pictures of.

Yet, every day, the officials would take her into a clean, spacious room and pose a proposition. "Now, Ahn," they would say, "If you will just bow down once to this Shinto religious shrine, you can be immediately released. We know it is because of this false religion, Christianity, that you did that thing in Tokyo. Just bow to the shrine, and you are a free woman." Back to the cell she inevitably returned. One day they took her out and laid this before her: "Ahn, just *promise* you will bow to a Shinto shrine when you are released, and you can go free." Shinto shrines were everywhere in those days, sometimes even nailed to trees in the forest. No one need ever see or know. But she replied, "For a Christian to make a promise is the same as doing it." Back to the cell again. She would not deny Christ, at any cost.

This pattern persisted for days, weeks, months, years. The fact that she lived was a miracle of God.

One night one of the guards she had won to Christ came to her. She had won many to faith in Jesus Christ. They conducted daily Bible reading and prayer in the cell. No copy of the Word of God was to be found, but Ahn had done what the Scriptures tell us to do. She had hidden the Word in her heart (Ps. 119:11). So she simply quoted the passages and chapters she had memorized. Many prisoners were converted as a result, along with several guards. So this converted guard came to this dear saint and said, "Ahn, the authorities have given up on you. You are to be executed in the morning. But another guard and I have arranged for your escape tonight."

"Thank you for this gesture of love," she replied. "But look at me now. My health and all is gone. And if what you say is true, in the morning I will be with Jesus, well and whole. And I'll see my loved ones once more." With that thought, she drifted off to sleep.

When the morning sun broke in the eastern horizon, Ahn was awakened by what she thought was the singing of a Christian hymn. The first impression that seized her was that God must be taking her to heaven; she could hear the angels singing. *Imagine*, she said to herself, *God is not going to let the officials execute me after all. I am dying, and I'm going to heaven; hear the angels?*

Yet she felt around herself and discovered she was still in the same filthy, crowded cell. But she could hear a hymn being sung. The lovely sound increased until the halls of the prison resounded with song as the whole prison filled with singing Korean Christians lifting up their voices in that grand hymn God's people love worldwide:

> All hail the pow'r of Jesus' Name!
> Let angels prostrate fall;

Bring forth the royal diadem,
And crown him, Lord of all.
(Edward Perronet, "All Hail the Power of Jesus' Name")

That very hour the news had come: Japan had fallen, the war was over, and she went forth a free woman. God even restored her health and gave her children. *That is victory.*

So rest assured, struggling child of God. What the Holy Spirit did for Ahn Kim in her circumstances, he can surely do for you and yours. He can meet every need. There is glorious victory in Jesus Christ.

## The Answer

Canaan is revival living at its best—what all sincere believers desire most. How can one be transported to that blessed Promised Land? To enter the Promised Land is simple, yet so profound. Here is the open secret: Although there are many truths to realize, truths that will be fully explored later, we at least "cross over the Jordan" and *begin* the conquest of Canaan by an all-out, unconditional *surrender* to the lordship of Jesus Christ. Without commitment, one will forever remain in the dreary wilderness. The revived life is born in an abandoned life. This is where it all begins. Evan Roberts, John Wesley, George Whitefield, Charles Finney, Elvis Marcum, and a host of others discovered the fact that revival is conceived in surrender to the will of God. We have seen this so often—Oh! will we ever come to that place of commitment? We must if we would experience any kind of reviving.

Granted, when one enters Canaan, there is still "much land to conquer." Israel did not possess the land from Dan to Beersheba the moment God parted the waters of Jordan for them. It took many days and many battles. But they did begin by planting their feet on Jordan's banks in obedience to God's leadership. Surrender to the Savior gets it all started. Without that step, we remain at a spiritual standstill, doomed to the wilderness. We must begin. The Jordan will part the moment we place our foot on that bank of surrender.

Purge me with hyssop, and I shall
be clean;
wash me, and I shall be whiter
than snow.
Fill me with joy and gladness;
let the bones which thou hast
broken rejoice.
Hide thy face from my sins,
and blot out all my iniquities.
(Psalm 51:7-9)

# 3
# The Revived Life Is
# a Purified Life

The Lord blessed, *really* blessed! The setting was a small church on the edge of town. God had been probing people profoundly for several nights during the series of special services. Then the break came.

The concerned Christians congregated in a back room after the benediction. It seemed as though the air crackled with conviction and a consciousness of Christ's presence. There were prayers, broken prayers; tears, sincere tears; confessions, heart-searching confessions. The Holy Spirit had come mightily among us, and we knew it right well. The event was one of the closest brushes I ever had with a real revival. All experienced God "high and lifted up," with his train filling "the temple" (Isa. 6:1-2). And seeing him, we fell at his feet like Isaiah and cried out with the prophet, "Woe is me." Deep conviction overcame us all. When you see the Lord, you see yourself. There was a coming clean with Christ rarely realized.

Pathos filled the prayer of one teenage girl. It seems she had
gone with a high school group to a ball game some weeks
before. In the excitement of the trip, they went to a restaurant
after the game to celebrate. There she stole a saltshaker as a
souvenir. Just a prank, just a memento. It only cost a few
pennies. Who would care?

God broke her heart over that "little sin," however. She saw
that stealing is stealing, be it a thousand dollars or only a
thousand grains of salt. She tearfully poured out her heart to
God, saying, "Lord, please forgive me. I'll take it back if I can
remember where I stole it."

Now isn't that taking it all just a little too far? Not really! Sin
is sin. No sin is "little" or "big" in God's sight. Granted, some
forms of evil have far greater *social* consequences than others,
but rebellion is rebellion. Any sin can bludgeon one's fellowship with Jesus Christ and hence dam up the rivers of revival.
In the last two chapters, the fact that surrender to the absolute
lordship of the Savior in one's life is vital to a personal revival
was illustrated. But what about the personal sins that we
commit? How do they effect a personal awakening? That issue
must be squarely faced.

## Coming to One's Self

A great and gracious awakening, personal or nationwide,
always has at its core a coming to one's self in the sight of a holy
God and getting thoroughly right with Jesus Christ. A case in
point is the revival that transformed the Hebrides Islands in
1949. That outpouring of the Holy Spirit broke upon the Island
of Lewis in a most fascinating fashion.

A group of concerned Christian men had been fervently and
sacrificially praying night after night for months. The burden of
their incessant intercession centered in a plea that God would
visit their community with awakening power. After praying for

some time, a young man in the interceding group stood up one evening and said, "Brothers, this is so much rubbish. Could it not be that we—the ones most concerned for revival—are the very ones standing in its way? Are we those who are hindering the work? The Bible says, 'Who shall ascend the hill of the Lord?/And who shall stand in his holy place?/He who has clean hands and a pure heart. . . .'" (Ps. 24:3-4).

Those words had no sooner fallen from his lips, when God opened heaven on them in deep convicting power. All were prostrated before the radiant holiness of the sovereign God. Their hearts were crushed as they confessed their sins and shortcomings. Then God filled them with unspeakable joy. The revival had come.

They jubilantly made their way back to the village. It seemed as though they were walking on air as they entered the out-skirts of their small community. To their surprise, however, the entire village was awake, gathered at the police station. What could have happened? Had some tragedy occurred? On inquir-ing they discovered, to their absolute amazement, that at the very hour the Holy Spirit had descended upon them in the barn, he had likewise fallen on the entire city with deep conviction. People were awakened out of their sleep under the Spirit's probing hand. They dressed and went to the police station, inquiring how to be forgiven and saved. It may seem a strange place to gather, but this is how the Spirit of God displayed his power among them. Needless to say, before that night passed, virtually the entire village was converted.

That is revival; that is how in principle an awakening breaks in on a people. Putting sin right is how the work begins—always. If only we could learn how to deal with our personal sins on a proper biblical basis, then the reviving power of the Holy Spirit could flow like a flood.

Moreover, we all well know on a personal level that guilt, even over so-called small sins, can dog one's heels until all joy and happiness slowly bleed away from the Christian experience. A psychiatrist once said, "If I could rid my patients of their feelings of guilt, I would have very little business." Conclusion: no revival comes, certainly no joy, until sin is forthrightly and biblically addressed. Therefore, how to deal with the sin issue must become one of the Christian's most vital concerns.

## A Puzzling Paradox

This principle points out a very puzzling paradox in our contemporary, permissive society. The currently criticized "old-fashioned" ideas of sin, guilt, and remorse are by and large rejected as a mere hangover from the outgrown Victorian Age. Yet the psychiatrist's consulting rooms are jammed with people plagued with guilt problems. Of course, we can paste new labels on the problem, but renaming it does not solve it. There still remains that subtle mountain of guilt in the background that casts its shadow over every aspect of life. If we could only be brave and honest enough to face the realities.

Yet being honest with oneself, even for Christians, is hard. It took the fiery prophet, pointing his long bony finger of accusation in David's face and thundering, "Thou art the man." Seemingly, nothing short of that trauma could bring David to himself, and David was a man after God's own heart. The most difficult words we ever frame are those of the prodigal son, "I have sinned." But frame them we must, for "If we say we have no sin, we deceive ourselves, and the truth is not in us" (1 John 1:8).

Now, how does all of this fit into the pattern of a revived life? An in-depth study of the first chapter of 1 John will perhaps make this evident and provide some answers. In this powerful passage on sin and confession, John sets forth a number of principles on the revived, awakened life.

## Fellowship with Christ

The key phrase in John's exposition of an awakened daily experience of Jesus Christ is found in verse 7: "If we walk in the light, as he is in the light, we have fellowship with one another." "Fellowship" with God, as John expresses it, is his way of describing the fullness of the revived Christian experience. If we were to ask the apostle, "John, how does one get into the experience of a joyous, awakened life?" he would be quick to retort, "Get into the habit of *walking with God.*"

Several beautiful things immediately pop to the surface concerning the possibility of walking with Jesus Christ. John first projects the idea that fellowship with God is an almost unbelievable marvel. It is marvelous because of the fact that "God is light and in him is no darkness at all" (1 John 1:5).

The metaphor of "light" is often used in the Scriptures to describe the essential essence of God's character. It seems to refer primarily to his absolute, consuming holiness, for that is the basic characteristic of his personhood. The idea can be graphically grasped in an Old Testament experience. In Numbers 21, the dramatic description of Moses' encounter with God is portrayed. The context presents the Lord's servant as depressed, distressed, and dejected. He had endured for decades the criticism and constant complaints of Israel as they wandered through the wilderness of the Sinai Desert. Now he was at the end of his tether. He had arrived at wits'-end corner. In the distress of his soul, he prayed and cried to God something like this, "God, the burden is too heavy. I've come to the end." Then it seemed as though a faint light flashed in his spirit. He prayed further, "Yet, if I could just see your goodness. That would encourage me so. Don't send us onward unless I can see your goodness, your holiness, and *know* you are with us."

God, who is always gracious to his burned-out servants, answered Moses with words of comfort and strength. God said in essence, "Moses, I understand your situation. However, no one can look upon the holy Lord and live. Yet I will meet your need. You will know I am with you. I will cause all of my goodness to pass before you. As I pass by, I will put you in the cleft of the rock and put my hand over your face lest you look upon the Lord and be consumed. Then you shall see only my back as I depart into the Shekinah cloud of my glory. Your need will be met." We sing about that glorious experience in one of our great hymns:

> He hideth my soul in the cleft of the rock
> That shadows a dry, thirsty land;
> He hideth my life in the depths of his love,
> And covers me there with his hand.
> (Fanny J. Crosby, "He Hideth My Soul")

Moses came down from that exciting and encouraging encounter with the God of consuming holiness, and the Israelites were awestruck. Although Moses was not aware of it, the very skin of his face glowed with the reflected holy light of God Most High. "God is light and in him is no darkness at all."

Several New Testament passages also point up the marvel of what it means to walk with a God of "holy light." The Bible tells us our God is *complete* light. John puts it this way: "In him is no darkness at all." God is completely and unequivocally morally perfect. His righteousness is infinite and ultimate. Absolute holiness radiantly bursts from his presence. "God is light [complete light] and in him is no darkness at all."

The light that surrounds the divine Godhead is not only infinite and ultimate, it is also *unchangeable*. James wrote, "Every good endowment and every perfect gift is from above, coming down from the Father of lights with whom there is no variation or shadow due to change" (Jas. 1:17). The moral and spiritual tone of our personalities can climb to the crests and then dip to the depths. But not God. His holiness is utterly unchanging. There is no variation with him. He is the Rock. He remains always "the same yesterday and today and for ever" (Heb. 13:8). God is perfect, unchanging light.

Furthermore, Paul states that the Lord's holiness is *unapproachable* light. "The King of kings and Lord of lords . . . alone has immortality and dwells in unapproachable light" (1 Tim. 6:15). Today, as perhaps never before, a fresh appreciation of the sovereignty and majesty of this great God of light is needed. Sentimentalism about God as "the man upstairs" or syrupy singers who croon "somebody up there likes you" picture the God of unapproachable holiness on a humanistic level abhorrent to the Scriptures. God is light, and his holiness is utterly unapproachable by sinful people in the flesh. He is *holy*—complete, unchanging, unapproachable light.

Now this is the God who invites us to come and walk in fellowship with himself. A marvel indeed!

## A Disturbing Dilemma

Yet it is right at this point that a dilemma develops. God is holy light. No darkness can abide in his presence. No evil shadows can lurk where God walks. As light and dark cannot inhabit the same space simultaneously, holiness and evil cannot inhabit the same place simultaneously. Simply put, no one can walk with the God of light and still cling to evil darkness. It will not work.

This is the sting of the dilemma. God says, "Come walk with me in the light. Yet you cannot walk with me if you permit the darkness of sin to invade your daily life—*and you do!*" John makes it absolutely clear that sin is a very real part of our human experience, even as Christians. "If we say we have no sin, we deceive ourselves, and the truth is not in us" (1 John 1:8). That is the quandary that develops the devastating dilemma. God invites us into fellowship with himself but then says we cannot walk with him as we are. Talk about being impaled on the horns of a classic dilemma! Is there an answer?

Before seeking a solution to our disturbing dilemma, it may help to make a distinction between two key biblical words: *relationship* and *fellowship*. When one initially commits his life to Jesus Christ to receive him as Lord and Savior, a new relationship is immediately established. The new child of faith becomes a child of God. This God of consuming light becomes one's loving Father. One is born into the family of God. Moreover, that relationship can never be broken. The Holy Spirit invades that new redeemed life to set his seal upon the newly found relationship. God has accepted the repentant one as his own dear child, and no one is able to pluck God's children from his hand (John 10:29).

Moreover, the blessings of God just begin there. Not only is a new, rewarding relationship with God established, a fresh vibrant *fellowship* with Jesus Christ is set in motion. Jesus Christ the Savior becomes a Friend, a living, dynamic reality in everyday living. Fellowship with the living God becomes a glowing and glorious life-style.

The vital distinction between these two key words is obvious. The relationship established by God is a once and for all experience. Fellowship with Christ, however, must be *daily* maintained. In other words, although we do not lose our relationship with God, fellowship with our Lord can be disrupted. There is a definite difference between being a Christian and being one who walks in dynamic fellowship with Jesus Christ.

Fellowship fluctuates, and its instability is due to personal sin. Thus we are back to our disturbing dilemma. If we are to walk in fellowship with the God of light, the sin issue must be forthrightly confronted. We must never deceive ourselves about our sin and its devastating power to warp and twist and bludgeon our fellowship with Jesus Christ. To do so is to be dishonest with ourselves and God. John reminds us: "If we say we have not sinned, we make him a liar, and his word is not in us" (1 John 1:10). To summarize, sin severs fellowship with our Lord. Although our sins may not destroy our relationship with God, they make a walk with him impossible. Hence, our journey with Jesus is jarred, and our walk becomes very weary.

Most people are willing to admit they are far from perfect. But often Christians fail to see their sin as a real, pressing problem. We all tend to excuse ourselves, to rationalize, to blame others, or retreat into the fact that we are saved and our sins in that sense are forgiven. But if one does not come to grips with the problem, a walk in the light as he is in the light is impossible, an experience described in pious platitudes but not made real. In our sinful state, we will never experience the revived life.

How does one, therefore, deal with the problem of sin? The solution must be sought at all costs. Dynamic Christian experience is predicated upon the solution to the sin situation.

## The Answer to the Dilemma

All this emphasis on sin may sound rather negative, but it is not. John has not produced this somber picture with his broad brush strokes on blacks and grays just to leave us in our plight. He paints the panorama so that we might move from the despair of ruptured fellowship to the delight of walking in the light. That is positive indeed.

The fundamental truth that John projects as the answer to the dilemma is found in verse 7: "If we walk in the light, as he is in the light, we have fellowship with one another, and the blood of Jesus his Son cleanses us from all sin." The key phrase in John's statement is: "The blood of Jesus . . . cleanses us from all sin." This simply means that if we are to walk in the light of God's presence, we must be constantly cleansed by the power of

Christ's forgiveness. The force of the verbal tense John uses implies a continual, daily cleansing of sins by the efficacy of Christ's blood.

Too often, we confine the death of Christ as the remedy for the sinful life to the historical past, to the time when we were first saved and hence forgiven of sin. John makes it clear that if we Christians are to walk with God, as well as be saved by God, we must be constantly cleansed by the blood of Christ. The death of Christ is not applicable on the day of conversion *alone*. It is that to be sure; the Father-child relationship is established. But it is much more. His sacrifice is to be effectual *every day*. If our lives are to be continually revived through walking in fellowship with Christ, we must learn the centrality of *regular cleansing* by the blood of our Lord Jesus Christ. That is what dispels darkness so one can walk in the light, thus resolving our dilemma.

Most of what has been said to this point will probably find reasonable acceptance. Yet right here much nebulous thinking begins to creep in. We may agree one needs to be regularly cleansed. However, too few have seemingly grasped the biblical concept of *how* the believer is to deal with his sins in order that the blood of Christ may continually cleanse and thus keep one in revival fellowship with God. This idea must be investigated with the closeness and precision that is unveiled in John's passage. To get a good, firm, biblical, precise grip on the practical points of these truths is vital.

## Sources of Temptation

It will be helpful initially to probe into the sources of our temptation to evil. Where does all this allurement to sin arise? What is its breeding ground? The Bible lists three. First, Satan's influence intrudes into the believer's daily experiences. Satan and his hosts attack and wage constant war against the people of God (Eph. 6:12). The Bible is explicit and tells us he tempted our parents in Eden, our Lord in the desert, Peter, Paul, and innumerable others. We can thus be certain he will fling his fiery darts at us as well (Eph. 6:16). Whatever the adversary can do to lead one to stray from God, he can be counted on to do. The devil is a very real personality with very real power. Get ready for him and his onslaught.

Temptation can also come from the "world." The Bible uses this term in the sense of an evil system with its own humanistic, godless, materialistic standards. Hence, the world becomes a source of severe testing. This is why John warns Christians not to love the world or the things in the world (1 John 2:15). Paul urges believers never to permit the world to press us into its mold (Rom. 12:1-2). Yet it is surprisingly easy to succumb and set one's standards on the living level of the material world.

Finally, the Scriptures state that temptation can come from within one's own self. James said, "Temptation is the pull of man's own evil thoughts and wishes. Those evil thoughts lead to evil actions and afterwards to the death penalty from God. So don't be misled, dear brothers" (Jas. 1:14-16, author's paraphrase). Our own desires, our own lusts, our own selfishness many times get us into trouble. We cannot blame the devil or the world for every temptation. One must be honest and tell it like it is. We have an old, unrenewed mind bent to sin. Robert Robinson's hymn expresses it correctly:

> Prone to wander, Lord, I feel it,
>    Prone to leave the God I love;
> Here's my heart, Lord, take and seal it,
>    Seal it for thy courts above.
>    (Robert Robinson, "Come, Thou Fount of Every Blessing")

We will not escape that unrenewed mind until we are in God's literal presence. The principle of the unrenewed mind will be discussed in detail later. Suffice it to say here that we shall always be tempted. But there is a way to deal with it, and in achieving victory, objectivity and honesty about the problem are absolutely vital.

## The Avenues of Invasion

Another help in coming to grips with the sin issue is to recognize the means or channels by which it invades one's life. The Word of God is clear about this aspect of the problem also. John sets forth the idea that "all that is in the world, the lust of the flesh and the lust of the eyes and the pride of life, is not of the Father but is of the world" (1 John 2:16).

The desires of the flesh, the desires of the eyes, and the pride of life are avenues by which sin makes its inroads through one's unrenewed mind. The Bible bulges with the idea. Remember Eden? After Satan had cunningly whispered his tempting words, "the woman saw that the tree was good for food [the desires of the flesh], and that it was a delight to the eyes [the desire of the eyes], and that the tree was to be desired to make one wise" [the pride of life]. Attacked on all three fronts, "she took of its fruit and ate; and she also gave some to her husband, and he ate" (Gen. 3:6).

Even the temptations of the Lord Jesus Christ unfolded along these same lines, although he had the perfect mind of God. He was urged to change stones into bread. He was famished—he had not eaten for many days. The desire of the flesh was very real for our Lord; he was human as well as divine. Then he was shown all the glory, glitter, and glamour of the kingdoms of the world. What a dazzling sight it must have been! Satan attempted to appeal to this desire of the eyes, even with Jesus. Finally, the devil tempted our Lord to jump off the pinnacle of the Temple in Jerusalem. Some of the Jews of the first century had the strange idea that when their Messiah came he would float down from the sky into the Temple area. If they saw Jesus do that, they would surely make him king in short order. The pride of life was being appealed to. Of course, much more is implied in our Lord's testing, but these basic elements of temptation are obviously there. Jesus himself is one who in every respect has been tested as we are, yet without sinning (Heb. 4:15). If our Lord himself was so tempted, it will not be different for us.

## Manifestations of Sin in Relationships

Then it is most important to acquire a proper biblical under-standing of how sin exerts itself in life's basic interpersonal relationships. Sin impacts a person in one or more of three ways. In the first place, sin always involves one's basic fellow-ship with God. Second, however, there may be sin that involves not only the Christian and God but also affects an interpersonal relationship with another individual. Although every sin is basically an affront to God, at times other persons are drawn in. Third, there are incidents when sin not only involves one's fellowship with God, but it is known and open and thus encompasses a group of people such as the church. Sin is always specific and personal.

Christians, therefore, should never see their daily sins as a nebulous, indefinite whole. This tends to prevent one from dealing with the problem in God's prescribed pattern. Sins must be seen specifically and individually and related to life's interpersonal relationships. For Christians, sin as a nonspecific principle is not the issue. That aspect of the sin situation was confronted when one first met Jesus Christ. It is *sins* that are to be dealt with in God's prescribed manner. Sins must be approached as describable, datable, individual, particular sins. This is most important. As sins are viewed individually and

classified into one of the three interpersonal categories mentioned, they can be dealt with forthrightly and in the scriptural
manner, for the Bible approaches the issue on that basis.

One must face these realities if there is to be a move into a
revived life. There has never been a profound revival blessing
of God without specific dealing with specific sins as they relate
to one's personal life and relationships. For example, the great
Shangtun revival of 1927-36 in North China began when the
missionaries began to pray and face God on specific, individual
issues. It illustrates the point perfectly.

The story begins in the Chinese seaport of Chefoo. Because
of a volatile political situation, all the Baptist missionary per-
sonnel of North China had been gathered as a group to the
seaport city. Bertha Smith, one of those dedicated missionaries,
told the story. The passage is a bit lengthy, but it is so insightful
and fascinating this precious missionary must be allowed to
relate it in her own words.

> One of our number, Mrs. Charles Culpepper, Sr., had suffered
> much from optical neuritis, which had left only partial vision in
> the eye affected. A few months before we were called to Chefoo,
> the good eye began to cause trouble. The mission doctor in
> Laichowfu advised her to go to Peking for treatment.
>
> The Culpepper family went to Union Medical College Hospital.
> Due to the philanthropy of John D. Rockefeller, Jr., the world's
> best specialists were to be found there. The eye specialist at that
> time was from Vienna, Austria. He changed her glasses but gave
> no encouragement about an improvement in the general condi-
> tion of her eyes.
>
> During those days in Chefoo when we often had fellowship . . .
> and heard . . . how God had marvelously healed all sorts of
> diseases, Mrs. Culpepper started having eye trouble again. There
> was still no eye specialist nearer than Peking, which was over 200
> miles away. She did not believe he could do much for her, even if
> she could receive his care. She truly felt discouraged.
>
> One evening the thought came to her to ask . . . the prayer
> group to pray that the Lord would heal her. It was a very difficult

thing to bring herself to do, for she still had the prejudice which had been in her mind for years concerning faith healing. . . .

By that time some of the refugeeing missionaries had returned to the United States, leaving eighteen of us. Some of them said that miracles of bodily healing were granted to first-century Christians as a proof that Jesus had risen from the dead. Now that the New Testament was completed, God expects people to believe the written record. Others said, "My God shall supply every need of yours." Certainly this was a definite need with no human remedy.

Since praying for the sick to be divinely healed had never been in her way of belief or practice, Mrs. Culpepper had never studied the Bible from this viewpoint. It was really the work of the Spirit during those days that brought her life before her like a movie. She began to see her real self as God saw her. Only the power of the Holy Spirit could have given her strength to talk very frankly with her husband, confessing sins against him and others. Even greater courage was given her to say to the whole group that she was most unworthy to be one of their number.

She was not the only one who was getting altogether right with God during that week. All of us who expected to pray for the eye were doing deep heart-searching. We were calling upon the Holy Spirit, who is Light, to shine into the deep recesses of our beings, to reveal anything that he was ready to prune out at that stage of our Christian development.

When the day agreed on arrived, twelve were present in the prayer meeting. Dr. Culpepper read from the fifth chapter of James. ["Therefore confess your sins to one another, and pray for one another, that you may be healed. The prayer of a righteous man has great power in its effects" (James 5:16).] He did not try to explain it; he was not leaving out anything of which the Bible spoke. He then put some olive oil on Mrs. Culpepper's head and asked all to come up and lay their hands on her head and pray.

I had gone into that room, so far as I knew, absolutely right with the Lord. I would not have dared to go otherwise. But when I stretched my hand out to Mrs. Culpepper's head, I had to bring it back. There stood facing me a missionary with whom there had been a little trouble. In her early years she had been head of a girls' school, but for several years she had been teaching illiterate women to read.

I had been asked to serve as principal in our boys' school in Chefoo while the missionary principal was on furlough. I had majored in education, and by that time had had ten years' experience in teaching and thought that I was 'the last word' in education! I had recommended Miss Hartwell to lead daily worship in that school. After a few weeks, I asked another missionary to tell her that methods for teaching old women were not appropriate for high school boys. She was hurt, of course.

But what about my proud self? I did not have a particle of sympathy for her. Right there before everyone, I had to say, "Miss Hartwell, I did not have the proper attitude toward you about that school affair. I beg you to forgive me!" My hand then joined the others and we prayed.

Had I refused to confess that sin, and joined in the prayer with it covered, I believe that I would have hindered the prayer of the others, and the eye could not have been healed.

Because all were right with God and of one heart, heaven came down! We did not have to wait to see whether or not Mrs. Culpepper's eye was healed! We knew in our hearts that she would never have another attack. The Lord had heard the prayers of such human frailty and had performed a miracle in healing one whom we so loved! She did not put her glasses back on. While the sight was not restored completely in the weak eye, both were strengthened and not once has she had any more pain, though using her eyes steadily for reading and needlework.

Walking around the room rejoicing and praising the Lord, we were all on a mountaintop of ecstasy. Then I had to be the joy-killer. There came over me such a sense of our inconsistency, that I had to speak of it.

"What kind of missionaries are we?" I asked. "We have gone through a week of heart-searching, humbling ourselves before each other and before the Lord, in order that we might be altogether right with him, so that he could hear our prayers and heal the physical eye of one of our own number. Yet we have never gone to this much self-negation for preparation to pray for the opening of the spiritual eyes of the Chinese to whom we have been sent." Our mountaintop of ecstasy suddenly became a valley of humiliation. We all went to our knees in contrite confession for having been so careless as to have gone along supposing that we were right with the Lord, while holding all kinds of attitudes which could have kept the Lord's living water from flowing through us to the Chinese.

Within a few weeks we were able to return to our various posts of work. Everyone went back teaching and preaching the tragedy of sin in the life and heart of a Christian.[1]

This graphic story of Bertha Smith leads us to the heart of the issue—what to do in regard to daily sins that have bludgeoned and warped and twisted one's fellowship with God.

## Confession of Sins

In a word, the Bible tells us we are to *confess* our sins. John forthrightly states, "If we confess our sins, he is faithful and just, and will forgive our sins and cleanse us from all unrighteousness" (1 John 1:9). What does John mean when he urges us to bring our sins to God in confession?

At the very outset, it is quite fascinating to see the intriguing implications of the word *confess*. In the language of the New Testament, it is a compound word. John wedded two different words, and the union gave birth to a new, rich truth. The term is comprised of the verb *to say* and the prefix *the same*. Thus the word we translate "confess" in our English Bibles literally means "to say the same thing as" or "to assent to" or "to agree with." Confession means we "agree with" concerning our sins.

With whom, however, do we agree concerning our errors? This precipitates a further question: Who convicts one of sins? The answer is obvious: the Holy Spirit (John 16:7-11). The Spirit of God is the One who puts his convicting finger on specific and individual sins which have warped our walk with Jesus Christ. Therefore, for Christians to confess sins scripturally is "to concede to" or "to agree with" the convicting Spirit of God that some *particular* act of rebellion *truly is a sin*. It means to get out of one's own self and stand by the Holy Spirit, be objective about the issue, and agree with him. It is an objective standing with God against one's individual sins.

This precludes any sort of general, nonspecific confession of sins. For example, how often we simply pray, "Lord, forgive me of all my sins!"—and that's it. This is not the way the Bible says a Christian is to confess. And that is why there is often no assurance of forgiveness in our prayers. Such an approach to confession may be fitting for a worship service in a group, but in individual private prayer, this will never do. To confess sins according to John is to name them individually, agreeing with the Spirit of God that the particular act of which he convicts truly is a sin. No one commits sin as an indefinable whole; thus the confession of sin should not be done in an indefinable manner either. They should be confessed one by one and named for what they are. That demands honesty and objectivity, as Bertha Smith discovered.

Further, this necessitates lingering before God long enough to permit the Holy Spirit to search one out, convict of sin, and place his finger on those particular deeds that constitute evil. Moreover, we must forsake our sins in the context of confession. That goes without saying; we would hardly be eager to confess sins and maintain fellowship with Christ and yet find ourselves unwilling to repent and forsake that which has so injured our wonderful walk with the Lord Jesus Christ. Forsaking sins is presupposed in the biblical concept of confession. But having acknowledged every individual sin before God in this prescribed manner, the assurance is given that the blood of Jesus Christ thoroughly and completely cleanses.

## A Sin Account

Perhaps a personal experience here will present some insight to the situation. Bertha Smith spoke in our church after returning home from her missionary service in China and Taiwan. Her challenge centered on confession. In the course of her message, she urged us to make out what she called a "sin account." She instructed us to take some paper and in the left-hand column write several numbers. Then in the quiet of a secret place before God, we were to pray that the Holy Spirit would reveal every single act that was displeasing to him and was thus marring our fellowship with Jesus Christ. Then we were to write down every specific sin that we had never individually brought before him in prior confession.

Many of us took Bertha at her word. I attempted to follow her instruction by making out my personal "sin account." Even though I had known this principle for some years and had attempted to live by it, much to my humbling, the Spirit of God brought to my mind many unconfessed sins. The probing finger of God brought back to my mind sins I had committed months, even years ago. The Holy Spirit so searched me out that I had a very humbling experience before the God of Holy and Righteous Light.

I was honest, however. I wrote down every failure, one by one. My sins centered in lack of love for Christ, failure in prayer, and the study of God's Word. I had relationships with others that needed to be put right as well. Sharp words had fallen from my lips, and it was necessary to restore some relationship with others. Time would fail to set forth all of which God convicted me. Suffice it to say the Holy Spirit deeply searched me out.

After writing everything down, I presented them before God individually, confessed them by acknowledging with the convicting Holy Spirit that those acts were actually sins of which I was guilty. Then I claimed the promise of forgiveness in 1 John 1:9. Remember, John has told us, "If we confess our sins, he is faithful and just to forgive us our sins, and to cleanse us from all unrighteousness" (KJV).

The forgiveness of God is a marvelous experience. God has committed himself. If we confess our sins, he is *faithful*, faithful to his promise and his attribute of love, and *just*—Christ bore all the penalty of our sins—to forgive us of our rebellion and cleanse us from *all unrighteousness*. "To forgive" in John's terminology means to wipe out a debt. "To be cleansed" implies the blotting out of a stain. God will not only eradicate all debts, he will even blot out the stain of the memory that may drag one down into spiritual depression and guilt feelings. God forgets; so can we.

The blood of Christ is powerful and precious beyond words. What a liberating experience it always is when one comes before God with honest confession. A new fellowship with God suddenly bursts into one's experience and life glows. I commend the exercise to you; make out your personal "sin account."

## Other Implications

A secondary problem emerges right here, however. It has already been implied. What if some sins involve relationships with others as well as one's relationship to God? In such an instance, merely to confess them to God alone is insufficient to experience the full liberty of Christ's forgiveness. We should confess them to God; this is obvious. But in the Sermon on the Mount Jesus advised: "So if you are offering your gift at the altar, and there remember that your brother has something against you, leave your gift there before the altar and go; first be reconciled to your brother, and then come and offer your gift" (Matt. 5:23-24).

One cannot avoid the simple truth outlined by our Lord Jesus Christ: If one sins against another person and fellowship is thereby marred, restitution must be made to the offended person as well as to God. If one fails to acknowledge one's sin and seek forgiveness from those individuals sinned against (as much as is possible in the present circumstances and as God leads), then one cannot really expect deep fellowship with God or with one another. The revived had all learned that. So must we if we would join their ranks.

The first time the Holy Spirit bore home this truth to me was several years ago while serving as a pastor in a small church in Fort Worth, Texas. A young, deeply spiritual man preached on this theme in our church. The Spirit of God profoundly probed all of us. Many were compelled by the Holy Spirit to put things right with different people. I, too, had to acknowledge, much to my chagrin, that I had sinned against several individuals. To be honest with God and myself, I knew I should put those things right. It was difficult; pride dies hard. Yet I realized if I were to have real peace and live a revived life, I must follow God's lead. Soon I was seeking out one of my Christian brothers. My sin may not seem of the worst nature. I had just lost genuine Christian love and fellowship with him. I went to him to acknowledge my error and seek his forgiveness.

Another brother I thought I should speak to had moved away. So I wrote him a letter and frankly acknowledged the truth. God thoroughly searched me out. I even mailed some money to put one situation straight. But after all, this was the only honest, ethical thing to do. It was anything but easy, however. The Holy Spirit normally must bring us to a place of brokenness before God (Ps. 51:17) before we are willing to humble ourselves before others (Jas. 4:10). Still it is the broken heart that God can mold and form into the kind of revived life that will exemplify Jesus Christ; he, too, was a man of contrite, broken spirit.

Do not understand this personal biography as saying every-one should do exactly as I did. To force one's experience upon another is not very Christian. I simply share it to show how God's Spirit led in my life. All he seeks from us is honesty and a

willingness to follow his leading with true humility and brokenness over what has destroyed our fellowship with him and
others. We must let God lead each one of us individually.

Yet, if there could just be genuine openness among the
people of God, if we could but embrace one another in the arms
of contrite confession, our hearts would certainly be bound in
Christian love, understanding, and forgiveness. This would
revolutionize our homes, our churches, our nation, and our
world. If fellowship with God and with one another means
anything, it obviously means this.

Finally, there can even be times when sin manifests itself not
simply against God alone or against another single individual.
It may be open and known to others. Does the Bible say
anything on this score? James tells us, "Therefore confess your
sins to one another, and pray for one another, that you may be
healed" (Jas. 5:16). Does James mean to say there are times that
we should honestly and openly confess some of our sins to
someone or perhaps even to a group in the church? This seems
to be his clear meaning. This is *really* difficult. Yet, there should
be that person or group in the fellowship of believers with
whom we can be quite open, honest, and candid about
ourselves.

This is what is meant by the beautiful New Testament word
*koinonia:* fellowship. John uses this gripping word throughout
the first chapter of his epistle. It denotes a living, vital, open
fellowship and relationship where two parties walk together in
harmony, understanding, and love. The church should always
be such a fellowship of love and acceptance. If it were, we
would feel unthreatened when we open our real selves to our
brothers and sisters in Christ. If our churches were a genuine
caring community, we could drop our masks and be real
people. The reticence to honesty would vanish. This spirit
always emerges when a true revival breaks in upon a people.

The revived life is an honest, open life of fellowship with God and one another. At times I have seen God's Spirit probe so profoundly among his people that confession actually broke out in the entire church, and it was received in the true spirit of Christ's love. What a time of healing and fellowship it was. Many were so moved and transformed in the experience that they have never been the same since. This is the kind of community of faith God honors.

## A Caution

Care must be taken, however, that this openness never be allowed to degenerate into an airing of one's "dirty linen" before the whole world. Some have fallen into this satanic trap. Such an exercise can become very damaging to spiritual health and fellowship. I suppose there are some areas of our lives that only God should ever know. Yet at the same time, there is a need for honest openness among God's people, a need to drop the facade and be genuine. As a sensitivity to the Holy Spirit is developed in the fellowship of the believers, he will grant wisdom so that it will be clear what should be shared and with whom (Jas. 1:5). One would hope that all our churches could grow into such a dynamic fellowship of revived love, understanding, and healing.

Of course, if one's sins are so gross and open that reproach is brought upon the entire church and thus the fellowship of the church is broken, then forgiveness should obviously be sought from the entire congregation. This is what lies behind the principle of church discipline that many congregations have forgotten today. Furthermore, this is probably the real, scriptural meaning of a public "rededication." Sin is what causes the need for rededication. If that sin is open and reproachful, then it should be confessed and made right with God and the church.

## A Final Word

The final summary of the whole biblical presentation of confession is that sin should be confessed in the area of the offense. We simply need to get right with whomever we have sinned against and lost fellowship—God, others, or the church. Only then will true revival begin in one's life.

A revived life is a purified life. Genuine fellowship with Christ and the essence of the Christian community are thereby established. This is walking in the light as Jesus Christ is in the light and being continually cleansed (1 John 1:7). The price is high. But the blessings of the revived life are incalculably valuable. Revived fellowship with God is the prize to be sought at any cost. And there is another step yet to take in seeking a personal revival.

For this reason, I bow my knees before the Father, from whom every family in heaven and on earth is named, that according to the riches of his glory he may grant you to be strengthened with might through his Spirit in the inner man, and that Christ may dwell in your hearts through faith; that you, being rooted and grounded in love, may have power to comprehend with all the saints what is the breadth and length and height and depth, and to know the love of Christ which surpasses knowledge, that you may be filled with all the fulness of God. (Ephesians 3:14-19)

# 4
# The Revived Life Is a Spirit-Filled Life

Dwight Lyman Moody was one of God's great servants. History will never forget him. In the last century his effective evangelistic ministry spanned two continents. It has been said of Moody that he put one foot in America, one in England, and shook the western hemisphere for Jesus Christ.

Moody was a tireless worker. But in the earlier days of his Christian service, that is about all that could be said of the ardent evangelist; he toiled incessantly. God blessed his efforts; for he was honest about his sins, and he learned to walk with God. Yet, he had not taken that next revival step; he lacked a true anointing of the Holy Spirit to make his life and ministry mighty. That is a step God desires all his children to take.

The day came, however, when Moody met God in a powerful way. The journey to God's fullness was difficult for the zealous young man. The account of his spiritual pilgrimage to the Spirit's touch is challenging and fascinating.

During the Civil War days in America, Moody did a great work holding meetings and distributing Gospels and tracts among the soldiers and prisoners of war. He ministered not only in Chicago but on many leading battlefields of the Southern states as well. When the hostilities ceased, he returned to Chicago. There he went to work in Sunday School and Young Men's Christian Association work. Through his efforts in the Sunday School movement, the International Sunday School lessons were started. This method of Bible study is used by many churches to our present day.

Moody became prominent in the Young Men's Christian Association workers in America. In 1870, at a YMCA convention, he first met Ira David Sankey, who became his famous singing partner.

In 1867, Moody traveled to Great Britain. He intended to study the methods of Christian work employed in England. He was especially anxious to hear Charles Haddon Spurgeon, the great English preacher. He also wanted to meet George Muller who had founded on faith alone a large orphanage at Bristol. Moody was then unknown in England.

During that first visit to Britain, Moody met Mr. Henry Varley, a well known nineteenth-century evangelist. As they sat together on a seat in a public park in Dublin, Varley said to the American evangelist, "The world has yet to see what God will do with and for and through and in and by the man who is fully consecrated to him." *He said a man*, thought Moody, *he did not say a great man, nor a learned man, nor a smart man, but simply a man. I am a man, and it lies with the man himself whether he will or will not make that entire and full consecration. I will try my utmost to be that man.*

Moody's hunger for a deeper experience of God was aided by the preaching of Henry Moorehouse, another famous English preacher. He came to Moody's church in Chicago soon after Mr.

Moody returned to America and preached. For a solid week, every night, Moorehouse spoke from the text John 3:16, "For God so loved the world, that he gave his only begotten Son, that whosoever believeth in him should not perish, but have everlasting life" (KJV). From Genesis to Revelation, he demonstrated how much God loved the world. That preaching on the love of God changed Moody's whole approach to evangelism.

Eighteen seventy-one was a critical year for Moody. He realized how little he was fitted, humanly speaking, for his work, and how much he therefore needed the Holy Spirit's power. This realization was heightened by two ladies who sat on the front pew of his church every time he preached. Moody was a pastor at the time. At the close of the service, they would say to him, "We have been praying for you." "Why don't you pray for the people?" Mr. Moody would ask. "Because you need the power of the Spirit," was the reply. "I need the power! Why?" said he.

In relating the incident afterwards, he stated,

> I thought I had the power. I had the largest congregation in Chicago, and there were many conversions. I was in a sense satisfied. But right along those two godly women kept praying for me, and their earnest talk about anointing for special service set me thinking. I asked them to come and talk with me, and they poured out their hearts in prayer that I might receive the filling of the Holy Spirit. There came a great hunger into my soul. I did not know what it was. I began to cry out as I never did before. I really felt that I did not want to live if I could not have this power for service.

Right at that stage, the great Chicago fire wiped out both Farwell Hall and the Illinois Street Church sanctuary: D. L. Moody's buildings. Moody journeyed to New York City to collect funds for the sufferers from the Chicago fire, but inwardly he was crying out for power from on high. The old ladies' prayers had caught up with him. Moody related,

> My heart was not in the work of begging. I could not appeal. I was crying all the time that God would fill me with his Spirit. Well, one day, in the city of New York—oh, what a day!—I cannot describe it, I seldom refer to it; it is almost too sacred an experience to name. Paul had an experience of which he never spoke for fourteen years. I can only say that God revealed himself to me, and I had such an experience of his love that I had to ask him to stay his hand. I went to preaching again. The sermons were not different; I did not present any new truths, and yet hundreds were converted. I would not now be placed back where I was before that blessed experience if you should give me all the world it would be as the small dust of the balance.[1]

## Is It Correct?

Moody had a life-changing experience. It comes over in principle much like that of Roberts, Wesley, Finney, and others we have previously encountered. Now is the time to ask: Is such an encounter legitimate? Obviously, I assumed in the first chapter it was. But is it really? We would all agree that such an experience can be justified *only* if it emerges from the Bible. Does the Word of God truly set forth the idea of "being filled with the Spirit"? That is the question. This calls for an in-depth study of the Scriptures to attempt to justify the position, at least as far as this limited space allows.

As one approaches the biblical basis of the doctrine of the Holy Spirit, the Book of Acts comes vividly alive. In Acts 2, as previously pointed out, there is a graphic account of the miraculous giving of the Holy Spirit on the day of Pentecost. What a dynamic day it was!

To understand clearly what precipitated this historic event, it is necessary to turn back to chapter 1, where Luke the author outlines Christ's compelling commission to his disciples. The

Lord said they were to proclaim the good news to nothing less than the entire world (Acts 1:8). A staggering commission! How could a mere handful of men and women of such limited resources possibly grapple with such a Herculean task? It's mind-boggling.

## It Is Possible!

Our Lord realized the commission was humanly impossible. So he prefaced his commission with the words, "You shall receive power when the Holy Spirit has come upon you" (Acts 1:8). This promise was further fortified by our Lord as recorded in Luke's Gospel: "I send the promise of my Father upon you; but stay in the city, until you are clothed with power from on high" (Luke 24:49, RSV).

These promises utterly revolutionize the entire scene. God's Holy Spirit of power would fall upon the disciples in over-whelming might. Because of that experience, the task of world evangelization could actually be fulfilled, staggering as it is. God would accomplish the universal work in and through the believers by the indwelling presence and power of his blessed Spirit. The disciples were to go back into Jerusalem and wait. In a few days, they would be equipped by God himself that they might fill their role in worldwide witnessing. They would soon be clothed with power from on high. After that, nothing could divert or deter them as they sallied forth to share Christ. Ten days later, Jesus kept his promise:

> When the day of Pentecost had come, they were all together in one place. And suddenly a sound came from heaven like the rush of a mighty wind, and it filled all the house where they were sitting. And there appeared to them tongues like as of fire, distributed and resting on each one of them. And they were all filled with the Holy Spirit and began to speak in other tongues, as the Spirit gave them utterance (Acts 2:1-4).

Many things should be said about this pivotal passage. For example, Pentecost reveals vital principles concerning evangelistic methods. Further, from this climactic event tremendous truths about prayer and waiting on God emerge. That dramatic day also demonstrates much about the doctrine of the church. For present purposes, however, we are compelled to confine ourselves to observing only two vital issues.

## Pentecost Principles

First, on the day of Pentecost all believers in the Lord Jesus Christ received the Holy Spirit as God's gift (Acts 2:38). Since that day, whenever persons put their faith in Jesus Christ as Lord and Savior, they immediately receive the gift of the Spirit. He comes and takes up residency in every true believer. This is why Paul told the Corinthians that their bodies were the temple of God (1 Cor. 6:19). No one is exempt. God's gift of the Spirit is for all Christians.

Second, these early believers were not only invaded by the Holy Spirit for the first time; they also received an infilling of God's power. As pointed out in the *American Commentary*, these first faithful followers had "a reception from the Spirit of extraordinary powers, in addition to sanctifying grace." In a word, they received the Spirit and were filled with the Spirit simultaneously. That should always be the pattern.

After saying this, however, it is very important that this particular passage not be pushed to extremes. Many have read far too much into these verses. Pentecost was unique. That divine moment was God's signal hour to pour out his Spirit on all flesh (Acts 2:17). Pentecost was the Father's day for the Holy Spirit to come and indwell and fill believers for the first time. Thus it was a singular epic in the life of the church. In that sense it is no more repeatable than the cross of Christ or the glorious resurrection of our Lord. This principle has already been touched upon. Yet at the same time, the passage surely implies that a Christian is to have a deeper experience of the Holy Spirit than merely knowing that Christ lives in one's life. Christians are to be conscious of the Holy Spirit's *infilling* as well as realizing he lives within. Pentecost forcefully projects that concept and conviction.

## Other Scriptural Truths

Principles of the Spirit-filled life are brought out with increasing clarity in subsequent passages in Acts. We read in Acts 4:31, "And when they had prayed, the place in which they were gathered together was shaken; and they were all filled with the Holy Spirit and spoke the word of God with boldness." Here Luke relates that the disciples who had shared in Pentecost again experienced an infilling of the Holy Spirit.

The events that precipitated a "second Pentecost" are noteworthy. Persecution had come to the infant church. They gathered together to pray for boldness to communicate Christ and his message. God marvelously met their need by once more filling them with the Spirit. Note: These believers already had the Holy Spirit in their lives. Furthermore, they had been filled with the Holy Spirit prior to the events recorded in Acts 4. Yet God met their continuing and deepening needs by granting them a fresh infilling of the Spirit. The obvious implication is that Christians need both the possession and the *constant* filling of the power of God.

The experience of Paul in Ephesus dramatically demonstrates another interesting account of the believer's relationship to the Holy Spirit. Acts 19 relates that the apostle met some people from Ephesus whom he assumed were believers. But he seemingly sensed something was seriously wrong in their lives. So he asked, "Did you receive the Holy Spirit when you believed?" (v. 2). In essence, Paul was asking whether their experience of the Holy Spirit when they believed was full and genuine. They answered, "We have never even heard that there is a Holy Spirit." This somewhat shocked the apostle and caused him to inquire further, "Into what then were you baptized?" In the baptismal instructions one would have thought they must have at least heard of the Holy Spirit. They told Paul they had only received John's baptism. So Paul informed them more fully about the gospel of Jesus Christ, baptized them, laid his hands on them, and "the Holy Spirit came on them" (v. 6).

Here is an important point: Paul was vitally concerned that these converts be fully instructed concerning the inner work of the Holy Spirit. Moreover, he probably saw the gift of the Spirit and receiving all his fullness as an experience taking place simultaneously with the moment of conversion. This is no doubt the way it should be. People being introduced to Christ ought to be led to seek the continual fullness of the Spirit as well as the abiding gift of eternal life (Acts 2:37-39). Why not present the full message to new converts? If they are ever open to all God has for his people, the moment of conversion is the time. Genuine New Testament evangelism demands this approach. It seems to me that evangelism of such depth would obviously solve many of the problems new believers so often have in regard to subsequent spiritual growth.

Paul's letter to the Ephesians presents another helpful insight into the concept of the Spirit-filled life. The apostle loved the believers in Ephesus. His ministry there was long and profound. It is, therefore, understandable why he prayed so fervently for them. The heart and essence of his pastoral prayer is recorded in the third chapter of the Epistle. It climaxes with the ardent request that they might "be filled with all the fulness of God" (Eph. 3:19). His fatherly heart longed for the beloved believers that they might continually experience all the fullness of the Holy Spirit.

Paul then went on to thrust home to the Ephesians the absolute necessity of the Spirit-filled life by commanding: "And do not get drunk with wine, for that is debauchery; but be filled with the Spirit" (Eph. 5:18). The apostle obviously expected the Ephesians to live out their Christian experience walking in the fullness of the Spirit of God. He saw no options. He had prayed to that end. Now he commands. Walking with Christ, in all his fullness, was not to be approached casually or only if it aroused interest. The New Testament word *plerousthe* (translated "be filled") means "you must be continually filled" with the Spirit. Paul's word is a positive command, just as the first section of the verse is a negative prohibition against drunkenness. Paul clearly saw the Spirit-filled life as essential.

## The Example of Jesus

As could well be expected, Jesus lived out his entire ministry in the power of the Holy Spirit. All he said and did was directed by and permeated with the Holy Spirit's presence and power. This is reiterated constantly in the Gospels. John put it this way: "For the one whom God sent speaks authentic words of God—and there can be no measuring of the Spirit given to him" (John 3:34, Phillips). Jesus was always full of the Holy Spirit (Luke 4:1). If Christ is our example in all things, and surely he is, then we should attempt to emulate him in his relationship to the Spirit of God.

Space forbids delving into numerous other New Testament passages which teach the same essential truth. Suffice it to say, the Bible literally abounds in examples regarding the Spirit-filled life (for example, Luke 1:15,41,67; Acts 6:3; 7:55; 8:17; 9:17; 10:44,46; 11:15,16,24). Conclusion: The overwhelming weight of the Word of God fully supports the theme that being filled with the Holy Spirit is a valid experience. Thus if we take the Bible seriously, we cannot sidestep the fact that God's intention for all his people is that they be Spirit-filled Christians. The only deduction that can be drawn is: The Spirit-filled life is mandatory. D. L. Moody was right on target in his spiritual quest.

## Historical Accounts

If the Spirit-filled life is a biblically based concept, it should be expected to surface in the course of church history, especially in the lives of those whom God used in significant ways. When delving into the experiences of God's great servants, constant references to the reality of the Spirit-filled life are found. Church history repeatedly attests to the reality of being "filled with all the fulness of God" (Eph. 3:19).

## Historical Verification

The early church fathers, Origen, Jerome, Ambrose, and others, talked much about the work of the Spirit in the believer's life. As the years of God's dealings with his people unfolded, giants of the Christian faith are constantly found emphasizing the theme. Leaders like Savonarola, Fénelon, George Fox, Madam Guyon, John Bunyan, Wesley, Whitefield, and a multitude of others give testimony to the necessity of being rightly related to the Holy Spirit of God.

The eighteenth century witnessed a fresh emphasis on the theme. No man in those days was more godly or significantly used by the Spirit than young David Brainerd, son-in-law of the great revivalist Jonathan Edwards. His testimony of the Spirit-filled life is classical. Biographer Lawson tells us:

> Brainerd, the consecrated missionary, endured almost incredible hardships while laboring among the American Indians; but he lived so close to God that his life has been an inspiration to many. His biography was written by Jonathan Edwards, was revised by

John Wesley, and influenced the life of Dr. A. J. Gordon more than any other book outside the Bible.

Such intense longings and prayers after holiness as we read of in the journals of Brainerd are scarcely recorded anywhere else. "I long for God, and a conformity to His will, in inward holiness, ten thousand times more than for anything here below," says he. On October 19, 1740, he wrote: "In the morning, I felt my soul *hungering and thirsting* after *righteousness*. In the forenoon, while I was looking on the sacramental elements, and thinking that Jesus Christ would soon be 'Set forth crucified before me,' my soul was filled with light and love, so that I was almost in an ecstacy; my body was so weak I could hardly stand. I felt at the same time an exceeding tenderness, and most fervent love towards all mankind; so that my soul, and all the powers of it seemed, as it were, to melt into softness and sweetness. This love and joy cast out fear, and my soul longed for perfect grace and glory."

Many were the manifestations of the Spirit in his meetings and during his numerous seasons of fasting and prayer and longings for holiness of life. He seems to have risen above the things of this world to a remarkable degree. In his journal of March 10, 1743, he says: "I felt exceeding dead to the world and all its enjoyments: I was ready to give up life, and all its comforts. Life itself appeared but an empty bubble; the riches, honors, and enjoyments of it extremely tasteless. I longed to be entirely *crucified* to all things here below. . . . It was my meat and drink to be holy, to live to the Lord, and die to the Lord. And I then enjoyed such a heaven, as far exceeded the most sublime conceptions of an unregenerate soul; and even unspeakably beyond what I myself could conceive at another time."[2]

That is what it is all about!

During the past century, another surge of interest in the Spirit-filled life emerged. We have already related Finney's and Moody's experience. There were many more. Dr. R. A. Torrey, Bible teacher and preacher, gave his testimony in these words:

Take my own experience. I had been a minister for some years before I came to the place where I saw that I had no right to preach until I was definitely baptized with the Holy Ghost. I went to a business friend of mine and said to him in private, "I am never going to enter my pulpit again until I have been baptized with the Holy Spirit and know it or until God tells me to go."[3]

Charles H. Spurgeon, no doubt the greatest of all Victorian preachers, on one occasion quoted in a sermon Luke 11:13: "If you then, who are evil, know how to give good gifts to your children, how much more will the heavenly Father give the Holy Spirit to those who ask him!" Spurgeon then cried out to the eager congregation,

> O, let us ask Him at once with all our hearts. Am I not so happy as to have in this audience some who will immediately ask? You that are the children of God—to you is this promise specially made. Ask God to make you all the Spirit of God can make you, not only a satisfied believer who is drunk from self, but a useful believer who overflows his neighborhood with blessing.

The emphasis did not end with the closing of the nineteenth century. Many contemporary Christians are urging believers to seek the blessing. I will never forget hearing a great man of God at a large Texas rally preaching on the subject of the Spirit-filled life. At the climax of his message he said, "I do not care what you call it, the infilling, the baptism, the second blessing, or whatever. The issue is, have you experienced it?" This statement of the preacher may not be exactly *theologically* precise— and one should be careful and correct in expressing spiritual realities. Probably the preacher should have stated it in more biblical terms and called it the "filling" (I prefer to translate the Greek with *infilling* and do so throughout this book), as the Scriptures do. But what he wanted us to see was the vital importance of an all-out commitment to Jesus Christ and a touch of God's Spirit on our lives. That is the question we face. Are we living in the fullness of the Spirit of God? Few issues are quite as pressing as this probing query. Surely this is obvious by now, scripturally and historically. It has been stressed almost to tedium. But the rationale for all this emphasis is that only the fullness of the Holy Spirit of God can move one into a revived kind of Christian experience that our souls demand. Right at the core of every great awakening is a mighty outpouring of the Holy Spirit on believers. That is why it has been stated over and over again.

## The Obvious Conclusion

The fact of the Spirit-filled life should now be firmly established. To say it is not a genuine and essential experience is all but impossible. The Scriptures, as well as history, make its reality crystal clear. But what will it mean to our practical, everyday Christian lives?

First, the experience is vital to a healthy, growing Christian experience. This is true for several reasons. Not the least important is the fact that only the Spirit-filled believer can know the constant, conscious presence of Jesus Christ. Although our Lord never leaves his people, to be *conscious* of his presence, one must be filled with the life of the Spirit. Griffith Thomas, a British scholar, states: "The only true immanence of God is the presence of Christ by the Holy Spirit in the heart and life of the believer. . . . It is in relation to the Holy Spirit that the Christian doctrine of God meets the deepest human need."[4] In a word, the Holy Spirit makes the divine immanence an experiential and dynamic reality.

All this does not necessarily mean one is *always* emotionally aglow with God. One need not be constantly overwhelmed with the Spirit's *conscious* presence. Every Christian has dry seasons. When this occurs, it is the hour for faith to be active. If one is granted to bask in the sunshine of Christ's conscious presence, the Lord should be thanked for the warming experience. However, if circumstances, trials, or difficulties cast a shadow across life's path and God's hand seems hard to find, then the walk of pure faith is vital. At such a time, regardless of feelings, one simply claims the promise of his presence. God has said, "I will never leave thee, nor forsake thee" (Heb. 13:5). Thus keeping one's subjective feelings based upon the foundation of the Word of God we simply walk by faith, knowing he is always present, regardless of how we may feel at the moment. This is the kind of reality our spirit hungers for, and that is the kind of reality the Holy Spirit alone can give. That is why all true believers innately long to live in all his fullness.

The Holy Spirit not only makes the divine immanence real, he enables Christians to live a holy life. To talk about holy living may sound somewhat archaic today. Yet the Bible sets forth the concept repeatedly (for example, 2 Cor. 7:1; 1 Thess. 4:7; and Heb. 12:14). Personal holiness is not an outmoded idea at all. What is holy living? Living a holy life simply means developing a life-style pleasing to God and like God. "Be ye holy; for I am holy" (1 Pet. 1:16). All Christians recognize the inner compulsion to live like the Lord Jesus Christ. But more of that later.

Further, the importance of the Spirit-filled life is directly related to growth toward Christian maturity. This too is vital, and much needs to be said concerning the theme. But an entire chapter will be devoted to this issue later. Moreover, Spirit-filled, maturing Christians mean a Spirit-filled, growing, revived church. How desperately the world needs to see that kind of a congregation. But that has already been made amply clear.

Therefore, in the light of all that has been said, biblically, historically, and experientially, it is evident that God fully expects all believers to be filled with the Holy Spirit because it makes personal Christianity vital and alive. This is revival living at its height and *must* be experienced by all who would know God dynamically and make their impact on a very needy world.

Yet a mere casual look at contemporary Christianity demonstrates that considerable confusion persists on the subject. Therefore, before going any further, it should prove beneficial to deal with some of the current misconceptions that surround the principle. So many false ideas have grown up around the theme that many sincere Christians have been put off by the obvious error and excess. But we must not miss a revival blessing because of others who have perverted the truth. Let's not throw out the baby with the bathwater. So we begin by graciously, but honestly, attempting to clear away some of the underbrush that has sprung up in this beautiful garden of spiritual reality.

## Some Necessary Corrections

The first weed to be uprooted centers in the concept that when persons are filled with the Spirit they enter a state of absolute sinless perfection. This "experience" is often called a "second work of grace." The exponents of this approach describe a traumatic event, similar to the conversion experience, that blasts one into an orbit of perfection that precludes the believer ever sinning again. Yet this is obviously impossible to square with what John tells us in his first epistle—as we have already seen. To embrace sinless perfection is simple self-deception (1 John 1:8). To say one never can sin is actually to call God a liar (1 John 1:10). We must wait for heaven for that level of perfection.

Second, there are those who feel that the fullness of the Spirit must be accompanied by a certain gift of the Spirit. Usually the gift insisted upon is the gift of tongues: glossolalia. Let me illustrate: One night a friend called at our home. He is a layman and a very dedicated Christian. He had brought along a fellow layman whom I had never met. As we talked together, this new acquaintance asked me if I had ever been filled with the Holy Spirit. I told him, as unassumingly as possible, that I definitely had. My response took him back somewhat. He apparently did not expect such a positive answer. Then he asked, "Well, have you ever experienced the infilling with tongues?" "No," I replied, "God has not seen fit to bestow that particular gift on me." He then said, "But you *should* seek the Spirit with tongues."

I appreciated the man's zeal. I was grateful for his concern that all Christians become Spirit filled. His error was that he failed to understand what Paul forthrightly declared to the Corinthian believers. Paul told them in unequivocal terms that God gives specific gifts, "as he wills" (1 Cor. 12:11). After all, in the bestowal of his gifts, the Holy Spirit creates a body, unified and diversified. It would be a rather strange body if all had the gift of tongues. The body would be no more than one big tongue and therefore not a normal body at all. In a later chapter we shall look at the doctrine of the gifts of the Spirit in considerable detail.

In the third place, there are those who advocate that being filled with the Holy Spirit is always a very emotional experience. That growth of underbrush really needs to be eradicated. So many make shipwreck right here. Now it is true that being filled with all the fullness of God can certainly be quite emotional. It was for Finney, Moody, Brainerd, and others. Religious emotions are not wrong in themselves. They can be God-given and a source of great blessing. But it is an error to insist that being Spirit filled is *invariably* a great emotional upheaval. That is mere emotionalism. There is a world of difference between legitimate emotional reactions to spiritual experiences and simply drumming up religious emotionalism.

Further, everyone is a unique individual and thus reacts

differently to various stimuli. For example, some have a very moving emotional reaction at conversion. Others do not. We all recognize it as an error to insist upon certain emotional responses to the gospel. The same principle applies to the Spirit-filled life. Let the emotions be as they will. A changed and fruitful ministering life is what counts. As has been often said, it is not "how high you jump" when God fills you with his Spirit that matters; rather, what concerns our Lord is how straight you walk morally when you hit the ground. This has already been amply stressed in an earlier chapter.

A fourth false growth demanding at least a bit of uprooting declares that the more one subdues "self," the more God *automatically* fills one with his Spirit. This approach, if one is not careful, can subtly sidetrack a Christian from coming to a moment of crisis when once and for all he or she yields to God and by faith claims the infilling. It may be possible to yield to God unconsciously, but such an experience is rather rare. A moment of conscious crisis is usually important to most of us. At any rate, what finally matters is becoming obedient to God's will and a look of faith, conscious or not, for the Bible says God gives the Holy Spirit to those who obey him (Acts 5:32).

Another area of concern centers in the perversion of seeking the Spirit's fullness for some selfish reason. The blessings of God are never to be sought for any self-seeking end. For example, the Spirit's fullness is not given that we may be thought of as "first-class Christians" while others are inferior. Moreover, one must never surrender to the temptation to seek power in God's service so that self will be honored. Not only that, the Spirit is not to be desired so that one can indulge in a retreat from reality and live in some antiseptic ethereal realm of the Spirit that inhibits one from ever coming to grips with the blood, sweat, and tears of this world. God wants to be real to us, but not for the purpose of indulgence and misguided spirituality. *The glory and service of Jesus Christ is the only legitimate goal in striving for God's fullness.* This is the only motive our Lord honors.

## Biblical Terminology

Before passing to the more positive presentation of the principle of the Spirit-filled life, it will be well to pause and put the terminology on a biblical basis. Error in nomenclature can bring about error in thought, if not in actions. Earlier in this chapter I related the incident of a preacher who said it does not matter what you call the experience so long as you have it. In a sense, that is quite correct. Better to have the right experience with the wrong expression of it than *vice versa*. Yet, as pointed out, it is obviously best to keep one's terminology scriptural, not to be rigid or wooden in approach but to be biblically accurate.

This Christian life-style has been variously called the "infilling of the Spirit," the "baptism in the Spirit," the "second blessing," a "second work of grace," and so on. At the outset, terms such as "second blessing" and "a second work of grace" can be summarily eliminated. These words and expressions and the concept they imply are not to be found anywhere in the Bible. Being filled with the Spirit is far more than a "second blessing." Paul's admonition to the Ephesians in 5:18 is "be *continually* filled with the Spirit." Never does the Bible present the filling as a once and for all experience. It is a daily blessing to be enjoyed, a Christian life-style.

The terms *infilling* and *baptism* are scriptural, however. Is there a distinction to be drawn between these two words? In one sense, it seems sensible not to press a demarcation too far. There are times when the terms appear to come together in the Bible. In the bulk of scriptural references, however, there is something of a line to be drawn. The term *baptism* by the Spirit usually refers to the primary experience of being baptized by the Spirit into the body of Christ at the time of conversion (for example, Matt. 3:11; Acts 1:5; 1 Cor. 12:13). Baptism in the Spirit refers essentially to that initial reception of the Spirit of God at conversion, although this is no doubt a time of filling with the Spirit as well.

The expression "filled with the spirit" is normally employed by biblical writers to describe the experiences of those who are already Christians, that is, those who are already "baptized" with the Spirit. By filling the believer with the Spirit, God equips his people for service, ministry, and godly living (for example, Acts 4:8,31; 6:5; 7:55). But again, it is wise to guard against being legalistic on this point. Men like Finney and Torrey tended to use the terms interchangeably. Still, it seems best to follow the general scriptural pattern. This avoids confusion if not practical error.

## The Real Meaning

The positive side of the truth must now be presented. What does it actually mean to be filled with the Holy Spirit, and how does one experience it, thus moving into the revived life?

The essence of the concept can best be seen in Paul's oft quoted admonition: "be filled with the Spirit" (Eph. 5:18). This verse implies several essential truths.

First of all, Paul makes it very clear that the Spirit-filled life is a state as well as a crisis. A walk is implied as well as a dramatic encounter with God. Actually, the biblical emphasis is always placed on the daily experience and walk. As someone said, we are "leaky vessels," and we need a daily, fresh infilling of God's Spirit if we are to remain overflowing with his presence and power.

The proper spiritual stance is that as one walks with Christ, constantly coming to him as to a full fount, one is made full and running over with his blessed Holy Spirit. This is what Jesus meant when he said, "If anyone thirst, let him come to me and drink. He who believes in me, as the scripture has said, 'Out of his heart shall flow rivers of living water'" (John 7:38). The Holy Spirit who lives in the believer wells up within and simply overflows to quench the thirst of needy lives. Christians should be a constant perpetual fountain of God's marvelous blessings.

Furthermore, there are times when one must ask God for a special infilling to fulfill some specific task. These experiences have been called "anointings" for special service and ministry. The fullness of the Spirit is more or less constant. The anointing is momentary and unusual. This aspect of the Spirit-filled life is seen in such instances as Samuel anointing David so that his role as king of Israel might be fulfilled adequately (1 Sam. 16:13) and the anointing Jesus received for his messianic task (Acts 10:38). This approach is especially prominent in the Old Testament view of the Spirit's work. It implies special outpourings, or anointings, for differing tasks. We all need this sort of touch of the Spirit at times. This principle is vitally important. There are situations in which God would use us in a very unusual way. That is when we need an anointing. Most of us have probably seen this aspect of the Spirit's work in action. For example, when someone is declaring God's word, it seems at times a great outpouring of the Spirit descends. All are caught up in the glory of God. Probably all have been in that sort of setting occasionally. We should also earnestly pray for these special anointings. But again, one must not be legalistic in terminology. There are times when this phenomenon is called in the Bible "filled with Spirit," for example, Acts 4:8, when Peter addressed the leaders of Israel.

## A Summary

The entire experience of the Holy Spirit can be positively summarized as follows: As we walk in the light as he is in the light, continually cleansed by his blood, we come to him daily for the infilling of his wonderful Holy Spirit, thus finding life constantly overflowing with divine power. This is revived living, and this is God's marvelous way of being effective in service to the glory of Jesus Christ.

## How to Be Filled with the Spirit

The final question now becomes: How does one become immediately filled with the Holy Spirit? Five simple principles already implied should answer this fundamental question. They form the spiritual exercise to experience the Spirit-filled, revived life.

## Acknowledge

First, there must be an *acknowledgment* of need. If we are satisfied with our present spiritual state, little progress will be made in the things of God. The Lord Jesus Christ said, "Blessed are those who hunger and thirst for righteousness, for they shall be satisfied" (Matt. 5:6). If we have no real hunger for God or what he has for seeking believers, we should ask him to create such a desire.

There is so much to move one in that direction. There are tragic situations all over the world that cry out to be met in Christ's name. We cannot even begin to meet those needs in our own strength; we must have God's power. Revival will never come to our desperate society if Christians are not revived by the infilling of the Holy Spirit.

Something within us should yearn for all the fullness of God. The attitude of the psalmist expresses the heart of the earnest Christian: "As a hart longs for flowing streams,/so longs my soul for thee, O God./My soul thirsts for God,/for the living God" (Ps. 42:1-2). We must acknowledge our need.

## Abandon

After God has been able to create something of a genuine hunger and thirst for his best and having acknowledged one's need, one's next imperative step is to *abandon* all sins. To make a 100 percent break with all known sin is absolutely necessary. The confession of all known iniquities is the bottom line. This is not a call for sinless perfection. That has already been made abundantly clear. Yet, we can make a break with every *known* evil. We must strive to be able to say with Paul, "So I always take pains to have a clear conscience toward God and toward men" (Acts 24:16).

Is this asking too much? The Bible says, "If I had cherished iniquity in my heart,/the Lord would not have listened" (Ps. 66:18). Sin, unforsaken and unconfessed, severs fellowship with God, as already learned. One can hardly have Christ's fullness in one hand and grasp known sin in the other. Fullness and rebellion are totally incompatible in the believer.

## Abdicate

The next exercise is to *abdicate* the throne of one's heart. In the final analysis, we are forever faced with one basic issue: Will I control my own life or will I truly make Jesus Lord of all? We are forced to decide for one or the other. God's Word is very plain on this point. Remember, the Holy Spirit is given to "those who obey him" (Acts 5:32). Jesus must be Lord.

Many Christians seem unwilling to make such an in-depth commitment. Why? Perhaps we are apprehensive that such a decision will force us into becoming less of a real person. To give up ourselves to another—even God—appears to destroy something of our essential freedom and personhood. Yet nothing could be further from the truth. The devil's deception is what produces such a feeling. Actually, we become real persons when we yield to Jesus Christ. One is only truly "free" as the Son of God makes one free (John 8:36).

We also may fear that God will ask some terrible thing of us if we yield ourselves to his control. Never forget, however, that God is a loving Father. Understanding and compassion characterize our Lord. He only wants the very best for his children. His will is always that which brings fulfillment and meaning and reality to life.

Still, it is far from easy to yield one's self to Jesus Christ—even realizing all these truths. But God will help us even here. For example, one day a man came to a minister of the gospel and related that he wanted to be filled with the Holy Spirit. Yet he could not bring himself to yield to the absolute lordship of Jesus Christ. The preacher asked him if he were willing to be yielded to God if the Holy Spirit would give him the strength to surrender. The man replied he just did not know. The minister then asked, "Are you willing for God to make you willing?" The man replied, "Yes, I'm willing for that." So the man of God pointed the inquirer to 1 John 5:14-15: "And this is the confidence which we have in him, that if we ask anything according to his will he hears us. And if we know that he hears us in whatever we ask, we know that we have obtained the request made of him." They prayed that God would make the seeker willing to be made willing to yield himself to the lordship of Christ. He was at least willing for that to happen. They shared in mutual prayer, claiming God's promise that he would hear, for it was surely the will of God that his people be yielded to him. Then the power of Christ entered the inquirer's life, and he found that he could willingly present himself without reservation to God and seek the fullness of the Spirit. Perhaps that is where most of us must begin. Such a sincere prayer will surely be divinely honored. The Father will hear and enable us to make Jesus Christ Lord in the fullest sense.

## Ask

Fourth, after acknowledging need, abandoning sin, and abdicating control of our lives, we simply *ask* God to fill us with his Spirit. "If you then, who are evil, know how to give good gifts to your children, how much more will the heavenly Father give the Holy Spirit to those who ask him!" (Luke 11:13). God deeply desires his hungry-hearted children to come into his presence by prayer and ask him for this gift of the Spirit. He waits for cleansed, yielded, Christians to ask him for the Spirit's fullness. This is the essence of the crisis moment.

## Accept

Finally, having asked, we now *accept* the gift by faith and thank God for his goodness. We need not necessarily pray long and agonizingly. Acceptance by faith is what God honors. We accept salvation by faith and do not ask for any sign or particular feeling that God has genuinely saved us. So also we claim by faith the infilling of the Holy Spirit.

This is often something of a problem, however. It took me some time to see the reality of simple faith in receiving the fullness of the Holy Spirit. My heart had been hungry for God's fullness. The Holy Spirit had been exercising my mind for a protracted period on the issue. One night as the growing crisis developed in my life, I determined: *I will not go to bed until I am assured that I have been filled with the Holy Spirit, even if it takes all night.* I was at my wife's family home during a vacation time when I made that resolve. Already it was late, and the rest of the family had retired. Alone with God, I was determined to get the matter settled once and for all—at all cost.

Many factors in providential experiences had brought me to that critical point. I had thought, prayed, discussed, and read about the theme for months, even years. Now I was determined. I would not go to bed until I knew I was filled with the Spirit. At any cost, I wanted my life revived.

Yet pray as I would, the heavens seemed as brass, and no answer came. I suppose in my zeal I was expecting certain manifestations of the Spirit's fullness. I had read about the great spiritual experiences of significant people, but it was not happening to me as to Moody or Finney. So I prayed and prayed.

It was not long before I was getting into something of a state. Somehow or another my experience seemed to be empty and void; in fact, I was not having any experience at all as far as I could sense it. At that moment, my eyes fell on a simple statement in Torrey's book, *The Holy Spirit: Who He Is and What He Does*. He said if one had paid the full price of surrender and confession, all one had to do was simply to claim the promise. He emphasized that it was a mistake to look for a great emotional experience. Perhaps that is why I have so often stressed that principle in the earlier chapters. Suddenly the light dawned. The simple truth swept over me like rivers of living water. *That is it*, I exclaimed to myself. *The emotional response is irrelevant. As long as I am surrendered—and I have done that—God will surely meet my need*. How refreshing! The Spirit-filled life is there for the receiving by God's yielded people. I thanked him for his marvelous blessing of filling me with the Holy Spirit, closed my books and Bible, and went to bed. I was revived.

And what God has done for me and a multitude of others, he can and will do for you. The revived, Spirit-filled life is for every believer. Yielded, cleansed, filled! That was my beginning of a personal spiritual awakening. But there is more, I found, *much more*. To that "much more" we now move.

> But thanks be to God, who gives us the victory through our
> Lord Jesus Christ. (1 Corinthians 15:57)

# 5
# The Revived Life Is
# a Victorious Life

The abandoned life is glorious. Likewise, the experience of constant cleansing in Christ is truly tremendous. The blood of Jesus is precious beyond expression. Then to be continually filled with the Spirit is a marvelous way to live. But our experience of God is to go beyond the cycle of temptation, sin, confession, forgiveness, "refilling," *ad infinitum*. How frustrating running that treadmill would be. The awakened life is essentially a *victorious life*. Sin can actually be conquered.

## The Promise of Victory

The Scriptures are plain that God produces power over temptation to sin as well as granting forgiveness when we do lose our fellowship with Jesus Christ. There is victory through our Victor, the Lord Jesus. His promises of victory abound in the Bible:

> But thanks be to God, who in Christ always leads us in
> triumph, and through us spreads the fragrance of the knowledge
> of him everywhere (2 Cor. 2:14).
> For the law of the Spirit of life in Christ Jesus has set me free
> from the law of sin and death (Rom. 8:2).
> No, in all these things we are more than conquerors through
> him who loved us (Rom. 8:37).

Conclusion: In Christ the battle is won.

Few Christians seemingly experience that scope and quality
of victory, however. Believers so often grovel in the dust of
defeat that drains away all the joy and peace in Christ. Much
modern mentality among a multitude of believers is like that of
the early disciples between Friday and Sunday during that first
Passion Week: failing to realize that our Lord's death and
forthcoming glorious resurrection dealt a final, fatal blow to the
powers of evil. Why? The reason usually centers in either a
failure to face up to certain realities about the battle of the
spiritual life or attempting to achieve victory in a way that gives
no promise of achievement—or both. These two problems need
discussion.

## Two Pressing Problems

There is a deadly war to be fought. Paul put it this way: "For
we are not contending against flesh and blood, but against the
principalities, against the powers, against the world rulers of
this present darkness, against the spiritual hosts of wickedness
in the heavenly places. Therefore take the whole armor of God,
that you may be able to withstand in the evil day, and having
done all, to stand" (Eph. 6:12-13). Believers are engaged in
serious warfare. This issue must be faced.

When we face ourselves as we truly are, we become vividly
aware that there is a war within us. The mind of the flesh and

the Holy Spirit, both real parts of our personhood, are in a battle (Gal. 5:17). And the war is often rugged and rough. There is a mind in all of us that wars against the Spirit. Jeremiah said, "The heart is deceitful above all things,/and desperately corrupt;/who can understand it?" (Jer. 17:9). Our Lord Jesus Christ also stated, "For from within, out of the heart of man, come evil thoughts, fornication, theft, murder, adultery" (Mark 7:21). It is amazing; we can climb to the mountain heights of contemplation and adoration of God, and in a moment, plummet down to the muck of evil and lust.

The problem further compounds itself because human strength is seemingly powerless to do much of anything about it. It is right here that Christians often make the second mistake: attempting to gain victory along a path that is a perfect dead end. What are some of those humanistic traits?

## False Roads to Victory

The first well-traveled path that many tread, only to be disillusioned and defeated, is commonly called the "sinless perfection" route. There are those who have convinced themselves they are in a state where they can no longer sin. This error can be dismissed in just a word. Neither the Bible nor experience presents any validity to this line. Although there is sure victory in Christ, a perverted idea that in life we can get into a state where it is no longer even possible to sin is a delusion. These issues have already been amply discussed.

There is another erroneous road often trodden. It is characterized by a spirit of resignation to the "inevitable." Some say, "Well, if I cannot live above sin and God will continually forgive me, why get excited or unduly concerned about it? If I am under grace, I will not get uptight over the situation." But this attitude is as deviant from the divine plan as that of sinless perfection—perhaps even more. This approach has been historically called the heresy of antinomianism. We must never forget that sin is a real issue; it can damage fellowship with God. Paul countered this kind of argument forthrightly in Romans 6:1: "What shall we say then? Are we to continue in sin that grace may abound? By no means!" This detour will never direct us to our desired destination of victory.

Another route often run is the "suppression" syndrome. That is, knowing the seriousness of the sin problem, one ardently attempts to defeat evil with human energy, striving to suppress sin by one's own willpower. Many struggle on that stretch of road. Before I learned God's way of victory, I was running that route. Of course, I gained a certain measure of victory and blessing, but there were always those temptations I seemed powerless to overcome. I would pray about it; ask God for strength to overcome it; determine never to do it any more; I would even tell God that I would never fall again. I always left the door open, however, by praying, "by your grace I won't fall." I knew in the back of my mind I probably would. And I usually did.

No deeply sincere Christian wants to sin, of course. The Holy Spirit lives in our lives, and we know sin drains away his peace, power, and fullness. But evil constantly besieges the citadel of our high resolves until a breach in the wall is made and down in defeat we go once more. So we go back to God with confession and new resolves to do better next time, seeking a fresh infilling of the Spirit—only to repeat the same pattern over and over again. What a vicious circle!

The despair of it all: the harder we battle in our strength, the worse it gets. We finally get to the point of anguish and cry out with Paul, "Wretched man that I am! Who will deliver me from this body of death?" (Rom. 7:24). At that point of despair, however, there is hope. If God can move us to desperation and bring us to the end of ourselves, he may then be able to reveal his road to victory. We may well have to be brought to the place of absolute frustration before realizing that retreating into an unreal world of sinless perfection, resigning oneself to sin's captive claim, or striving to fight the battle in mere human strength leads to ultimate defeat. At that point, God opens marvelous truths in the Bible, pointing to the royal road of becoming a conquering Christian.

## The Prime Principle

John formulates the foundational principle of spiritual victory in his first epistle: "This is the victory that overcomes the world, our faith" (1 John 5:4). The beloved disciple is desperately trying to show us that *the way of victory is the way of faith*. That is the true path to becoming a conqueror. So vital is this basic concept that failing to grasp it will spell continual defeat in spiritual battles. In the final analysis, it is always unbelief, lack of faith, that forces one into the warfare of the wilderness (Heb. 4:2). Victory comes only through faith: believing God and moving into the "Promised Land" of victory. Paul presents the same spiritual plan stating, "Above all, taking the shield of faith, wherewith ye shall be able to quench all the fiery darts of the wicked" (Eph. 6:16, KJV). Belief is the basis of all Christian conquest. "Faith is the victory, we know,/That overcomes the world" (John Yates, "Faith is the Victory").

Dynamic faith must have an object, however. It will not do simply to say, "Have faith!" Such pious statements may sound spiritual and supportive, but they are too indefinite to possess any positive power. Genuine faith must always have its basis in objective reality: the truth of God. Truth as the object or ground of faith is to be understood in a twofold sense.

First, believers have the objective truth of God, the Scriptures. The Bible has its role to play as an object of vibrant belief. Second, Christians are also confronted with the living truth,

Jesus Christ himself. He is always the goal of our faith endeavors. Therefore, when it is stated that faith has truth as its object, it should be understood in this twofold manner. What, then, is the biblical truth concerning our personal experience of Jesus Christ that forms the foundational facts to place our faith upon and hence experience victory? That is the key quest. Paul declares the following spiritual reality:

> What shall we say then? Are we to continue in sin that grace may abound? By no means! How can we who died to sin still live in it? Do you not know that all of us who have been baptized into Christ Jesus were baptized into his death? We were buried therefore with him by baptism into death, so that as Christ was raised from the dead by the glory of the Father, we too might walk in newness of life. For if we have been united with him in a death like his, we shall certainly be united with him in a resurrection like his. We know that our old self was crucified with him so that the sinful body might be destroyed, and we might no longer be enslaved to sin. For he who has died is freed from sin. But if we have died with Christ, we believe that we shall also live with him. For we know that Christ being raised from the dead will never die again; death no longer has dominion over him. The death he died he died to sin, once for all, but the life he lives he lives to God. So you also must consider yourselves dead to sin and alive to God in Christ Jesus (Rom. 6:1-11).

Do you sense the significant impact of what Paul is saying? He begins by stating that if one is dead he is free from sin's power and dominion. Quite reasonable! When we die, we will have no impulse to sin. Yet if we are dead, we will be of no value to Christ's service on earth. If we could only be dead and alive at the same time, that would solve the dilemma. But that is quite unthinkable, at least so it seems from any mere human perspective. Few of us have seen any real living dead people. Right here, however, Paul startles us with a significant statement. He projects the principle that because of identification with Jesus Christ, whereby believers have been made one with him, Christians share in the Lord's death and resurrection.

## We Are Dead to Sin

We are to understand that salvation, as well as providing forgiveness *of* sins, also means we have died with Christ *to* sin through our faith union with the crucified Lord. In the spiritual sense—yet in a very real way—when Christ died on the cross, the "old man" died with him. When he gained the victory by his blood, we shared in that victory by death. Therefore, our old nature is dead, truly dead and gone, crucified with Christ. We really are new people. That is exactly what Paul said. And he meant it; it's true. The mind must still be renewed as we shall emphasize in a moment, but our "old man" is actually dead. As believers, it is not so much that we have an old nature and a new one, each of equal strength, battling one another. This idea is often held by believers. But we are to recognize that the "old man" has actually been crucified with Christ. This fact is hard to grasp intellectually; yet the Bible clearly teaches it. What is "old" about us is the as yet unrenewed or carnal aspect of our "mind." But more of that shortly. Hammer it down here that the "old man" is honestly and truly crucified, dead and buried with Christ. Do not slip into the rut of thinking that you, as a crucified Christian, have two equally powerful natures, one good and one bad. *The old man is dead with Christ.*

## We Are Alive to God

Furthermore, not only have we died with Christ and shared in that experience of death, we have also been spiritually resurrected with him. We live because he lives. Being "in him" when he arose, we too broke the bondage of death and came forth from the tomb. We are now animated by the resurrected life of our Lord in the person of the Holy Spirit. The gift of a new nature in Christ is ours; we are wholly new, born again. So we are dead to sin and alive to God. The old nature is dead; the new nature is alive. Can sin thus lord it over us? It absolutely cannot. We are dead to it and living the resurrected life of Christ. That is our birthright in Jesus Christ. As one writer expressed it, we are "born crucified."

The rationality behind these realities is that God sees his children as *in Christ*. The biblical expression "in Christ," or its equivalent, is used over 160 times in the New Testament. Believers are actually *in Christ*, in genuine spiritual union with him. He is not only in us; we are in him. That means, according to Paul, that what Christ has experienced, Christians also have experienced. Therefore, when Jesus died, if you are a true believer, you were crucified with him. Thus you are already dead. As a result you are freed from sin's dominion. Sin is no longer master; one's old nature has been crucified with Christ (Gal. 2:20). The concept of "in Christ" is the key that unlocks the treasure-house of the apostle's understanding of the whole Christian experience.

This fact obviously does not appeal to human logic. It is most difficult to realize these truths as we objectively look at our real selves. That is because we still have our "minds" to contend with. Before our conversion, our minds became so accustomed to moving us to act in the "old carnal way" that they must be constantly renewed. After all, we completely thought and acted as "old men" before being saved, being "crucified with Christ." It takes the grace of God to change that carnal way of thinking, feeling, willing, being—which is the function of the "mind" as the Bible uses the term. That is why Paul emphasized continually: "Do not be conformed to this world but be transformed by the renewal of your mind, that you may prove what is the will of God, what is good and acceptable and perfect" (Rom. 12:2); "and be renewed in the spirit of your minds, and put on the new nature, created after the likeness of God in true righteousness and holiness" (Eph. 4:23-24); "Have this mind among yourselves, which is yours in Christ Jesus" (Phil. 2:5). "Whatever is true, . . . pure, . . . lovely. . . think about these things" (Phil. 3:8). As the Old Testament writer put it: "As he thinketh in his heart, so is he" (Prov. 23:7). The mind, the core of conscious acting, is central and must be dealt with by the renewing power of the Holy Spirit. This mind-renewing process the Bible calls *sanctification*. It is a lifelong process.

Only faith can grasp all these tremendous truths of what it means to be "in Christ." But *therein lies the victory*. As one author has pointedly expressed it:

> . . . when Christ died on the cross to sin, we were identified with Him in that death to sin. That is, we died *with* Him. By our union with Him in His death, we were freed from sin and the penalty of sin and emancipated from the power of sin. All our sanctification, therefore, must be traced to, and rest upon, the atoning sacrifice of our Lord Jesus Christ. The cross of Christ is the efficient cause of deliverance from the power of sin. Freedom from the dominion of sin is a blessing we may claim by faith, just as we accept pardon.[1]

## The Practicalities

The principle works beautifully in everyday life. Here is how the Holy Spirit actualizes it in our experience: Let us say that we are confronted by one of our old weaknesses. The unrenewed mind, accustomed to foster the things of the flesh, exerts itself. "Here we go again," we say. The battle to overcome the temptation has been fought and lost so often. But now we recognize the reason the temptation has an appeal is because of the old, yet unrenewed part of our mind. That is what moves us to think, feel, and decide contrary to God's purpose. Then the new truth of the Bible is pressed home to our consciousness by the Holy Spirit. Realizing our identification with Christ in his death and resurrection, and by faith in that biblical reality, we confront the temptation and retort, *This sin has no more power over me. I am dead to it. I am a new person. The old nature is crucified. I am alive to God, and the resurrected life of Jesus Christ is mine.* We take the ground of faith and stand against the temptation. Thus trusting Christ's promise, we look to God and his power for the victory. Faith in the fact of one's death to sin, and a vital look in faith to God, is the answer. That act of faith involves the twin aspects of the grounds for belief: the Bible and our powerful Lord.

There is a battle, of course. But the battle is not to fight sin directly. That spells certain defeat. Sin is stronger than we are. We dare not fight Satan on his own ground. He is surely mightier than we. The war to be fought is to strive to stay in *the field of faith*. The battle is the Lord's (2 Chron. 20:15). There, in faith, we rest. How Satan loves to deceive us here! The devil will do anything and everything to get us to surrender our position of faith. As one author has put it: "His aim is to get the believer to forsake faith's position . . . for the moment the believer quits faith's position, he falls under Satan's power. Hence the fight is not merely 'the good fight' . . . but the good fight *of faith*" (1 Tim. 6:12).[2]

Thus we take our stand on faith. This is the only way to defeat "the wiles of the devil" (Eph. 6:11) and be victorious. We do not work toward victory. By faith we work from it as already ours in Christ. We are new people—righteous before God in Christ. Consequently, we live and battle in a new arena, an arena of the freedom of faith. This is the victory. Not only in eternity are we delivered from the penalty and presence of sin, but now by faith we are saved from its power. Deliverance from sin's dominance is as much a part of salvation as deliverance from its penalty. All of these beautiful realities are wrapped up in our conversion experience. We need to know we are accepted by God in Christ and a whole new nature is ours. We are righteous in Christ. Therefore, we permit the Holy Spirit to renew our minds constantly, and sanctification just naturally follows. Redemption is as much in the present tense as in the past or the future.

## Another Approach

Perhaps the principle can be further illustrated this way: There are two laws that clamor for ascendancy in the Christian's life. One is the "law of sin and death" (Rom. 8:2) that operates through the unrenewed mind—already amply discussed. The law of sin functions in and through us constantly if we give it ascendancy through lack of surrender to Jesus Christ and his daily lordship in our lives, or if we fail to recognize that our "old man" is dead in Christ. The other is the "law of the Spirit of life in Christ Jesus" (Rom. 8:2). This law works through our new, redeemed nature as the new mind is constantly renewed and enlarged. In this latter law lies the victory.

We can liken the interaction of these two principles to ascending into the skies in a balloon. The law of sin functions like the law of gravity. Its pull cannot be escaped. Still, the balloon ascends. How? Because of a higher law counteracting the law of gravity. The gas in the balloon is more powerful than the downward pull. In like fashion, the law of the Spirit of life in Christ Jesus is a higher law that overcomes the tendency of the unrenewed mind. As we permit it by faith to function in our lives, we can ascend to spiritual heights. As the new nature ascends, our minds are constantly renewed into Christlikeness. "There is therefore now no condemnation for those who are in Christ Jesus. For the law of the Spirit of life in Christ Jesus has set me free from the law of sin and death" (Rom. 8:1-2).

Moreover, the wind of the Spirit carries us along over obstacles in the way God would have us to travel.

Two or three insights emerge out of the above analogy. First, the old mind that is open to the law of sin and death is to some extent always present with us. It is never entirely eliminated. Absolute, complete sanctification waits for us in heaven. Second, the law of the Spirit of life in Christ Jesus overcomes, or counteracts, the downward pull of the law of sin and death because of its greater power. This process cultivates the new mind of Christ in us. If the higher law ever ceases to be operative in experience, we fall to earth again. So the Christian must stay "in the balloon," that is, in the arms of trusting, ascending faith in our identification "in Christ." Thus the mind is constantly renewed, and the process of sanctification moves along.

Therefore, by faith Christians reckon themselves dead to sin and alive to God through identifying with Christ. As a consequence, they yield themselves to God and look to him for victory. That is where the decision-making element resides. That is where willpower is exercised. Deciding to yield to Christ and operate on the basis of faith is the issue. He *must* be in control of our lives. Then, in faith, we constantly identify with Christ and his resurrection. John was right. "This is the victory that overcomes the world, our faith" (1 John 5:4). The Holy Spirit works in all believers according to their faith and will orchestrate genuine Christian victory in every area of life.

I remember well when these refreshing truths first began to dawn on me. I had been a battling believer for many years and had fought many a skirmish—and lost several. I had eaten my share of manna in the wilderness, but my heart was hungry for the milk and honey of Canaan. Some friends were traveling with my wife and me to a Christian assembly some distance from our home. On the way, we stopped at a little rural church to attend an evening service. The young pastor was a mutual acquaintance, and although we did not know him too well we invited him to join us. He consented to come along. God had something in store for us all—something of which we had no idea when we made that simple invitation.

This young minister truly knew God. We began fellowshipping over the things of Christ, and what a time in the Lord we had! As he shared what God had taught him, it was like sitting at a cool fountain in a dreary desert land. We were all wonderfully refreshed. We stayed up night after night, after the evening assembly meetings, just drinking in what God had for us. I learned more about the victorious life in those few days than in any period of my Christian experience. God taught me the joy of knowing that I had been crucified with Christ, yes, had been resurrected with him. Those days will always be remembered with gratitude to God. A new life of victory had been opened.

## The Normal Christian Life

This quality of living is not to be thought of as unusual for the Christian. As one writer puts it, it is just the "normal Christian life." Being crucified with Christ and raised to walk in newness of life is not a position one attains by ardent spiritual striving. It is not the end result of much maturing and gigantic growing in Christ. This marvelous position all believers hold by virtue of the fact of being born again by the grace of God and possessed by the Holy Spirit. Again let it be emphasized, *every believer* is "born crucified." The Christians' part is merely to appropriate by faith what is already theirs and start living like it. God accepts you. As Paul says: "I have been crucified with Christ; it is no longer I who live, but Christ who lives in me; and the life I now live in the flesh I live by faith in the Son of God, who loved me and gave himself for me" (Gal. 2:20). This is a wonderful reality. Do not permit yourself to be maneuvered off the ground of faith and start striving in the flesh. Stay on the principle of trust. But make no mistake about it, to remain on faith's ground demands some discipline.

## Abiding in Christ

The secret of standing on the ground of faith is learning to abide in Christ (John 15). Therefore, we must obviously learn the discipline of abiding in our powerful Lord. As Griffith-Thomas expressed it, "Let all your enthusiasm be put into abiding."

## The Resource of the Bible

If we are to abide in Christ and thus plant our feet firmly on the ground of faith, Bible study is vital. This is the first discipline. One can never live the revived life apart from a consistent study of the Word of God. Paul's makes this very clear when he says, "So then faith cometh by hearing, and hearing by the word of God" (Rom. 10:17). A vibrant, revived faith develops from the assimilation of God's truth in the Word.

After all, did not our Lord Jesus Christ himself rely upon the Scriptures during his testing time in the wilderness? In the temptation narratives in Matthew and Luke, Jesus defeated the devil by his skillful use of the Word of God. In like manner, the Scriptures will do several things for us during our testing times.

First, the Bible helps one recognize the enemy. To identify the foe is not always easy. Satan can appear even "as an angel of light" (2 Cor. 11:14). There is wisdom in that tactic, of course. If the devil were to come and say, "I'm the old serpent, and I want you to do thus and so," few would listen. He is well aware of that fact; so he creeps in very craftily and whispers, "I am the voice of God, and here is what he wants you to do." How subtle! But if we are alive to the truth of God's Word, we know the Holy Spirit *never* leads one into any act that is contradictory to the Scriptures or that will fail to glorify Jesus Christ. Thus we have a valuable tool to enable us to identify the source of the many voices that crowd in on us.

Second, as implied above, the Bible instructs believers in discerning the will of God. The leadership of the Holy Spirit comes by understanding the Word of Christ. In the third temptation of Jesus, Satan attempted to lead our Lord astray by quoting the Scriptures himself. However, he applied it incorrectly. Our Lord turned the situation around and once again defeated him by appealing to the Word of God and interpreting and applying it properly. Remember Paul's instruction to Timothy: "Rightly dividing the word of truth" (2 Tim. 2:15).

Finally, the Bible inspires, strengthens, and develops one's faith. Through the Scriptures, Christians learn of their identification with Christ in his death and resurrection. Therefore, the more we study, the deeper these truths are impressed upon us and the more we learn to rest upon them. Faith is the victory that overcomes the world, and from the Bible we are made aware of the resources that are ours in Jesus Christ. Thus we are made bold to claim all God has said. Faith is what takes hold on God's promises in the Scriptures and fills life with victory.

## The Place of Prayer

God has given the marvelous resource of prayer in abiding in Christ. Prayer opens the portals to God who has all power. Little wonder believers are urged to "Pray without ceasing" (1 Thess. 5:17). Prayer is not a mere psychological exercise to change *us*. It does that, but far more takes place when God's people truly pray. God genuinely *answers* prayer. Things happen that would not have happened if sincere and scriptural prayer had not been offered. How often we would be utterly lost and in despair were it not for the rescuing hand of God in answer to prayer. Every need of life can be met by God. Moreover, the Father longs for us to come to him and lay our concerns and cares at his feet. He invites us to "boldly approach the throne of our gracious God, where we may receive mercy and in his grace find timely help" (Heb. 4:16, NEB).

What is prayer? In simplest terms, it is just conversing with God. As Rosalind Rinker puts it, "Prayer is the expression of the human heart in conversation with God. The more the natural the prayer, the more real He becomes. It has all been simplified for me to this extent: prayer is a dialogue between two persons who love each other."[3] Abiding in Christ means living with him and loving him. And surely we converse with those with whom we live in a deep love relationship. We share our cares, our ambitions, our frustrations, our very lives. This is what prayer is all about; we share with God. It is vital to abiding victory in Christ. The revived life begins, is permeated with, and culminates in a life of prevailing, passionate, personal prayer.

Profitable prayer is not easy, however. To develop a genuine prayer life takes concerted effort. Perhaps I should only speak for myself, but I find I must constantly discipline myself if I am to develop any kind of a regular prayer life. We must pray regardless of circumstances, feelings, or any situation in which we find ourselves.

Some time ago I was privileged to conduct a conference for college students on prayer and evangelism. In the course of the many discussions on those two vital topics, someone offered the opinion that prayer should only be made when one is moved by circumstances to pray. I strongly disagreed. Circumstances are usually not very conducive to prayer, at least until we get into real trouble. But prayer should not always grow out of panic situations. If we let circumstances dictate our prayer life, we may never get around to the abiding aspect of prayer. Then when things do go wrong, it is a frantic search to try and find God. No, we must discipline ourselves and develop regular times to come before God's throne of grace. Revived living abides in Christ. And abiding in Christ is utterly dependent on prayer. We shall see this in more depth in a later chapter.

## The Resources of the Christian Armor

To bring this chapter on revival victory to a close, one final look must be given to the resources found in donning the "whole armor of God." Any soldier needs equipment to fight successfully. In achieving victory in Christ, the same principle holds. Paul shares what this "whole armor of God" consists of:

> Finally, be strong in the Lord and in the strength of his might. Put on the whole armor of God, that you may be able to stand against the wiles of the devil. For we are not contending against flesh and blood, but against the principalities, against the powers, against the world rulers of this present darkness, against the spiritual hosts of wickedness in the heavenly places. Therefore take the whole armor of God, that you may be able to withstand in the evil day, and having done all, to stand. Stand therefore, having girded your loins with truth, and having put on the breastplate of righteousness, and having shod your feet with the equipment of the gospel of peace; besides all these, taking the shield of faith, with which you can quench all the flaming darts of the evil one. And take the helmet of salvation, and the sword of the Spirit, which is the word of God (Eph. 6:10-17).

Each piece of the Christian's protective armor is essential. First, believers are to be girded "about with truth." That means living lives of genuine honesty. Whenever any Christians get "unreal" about themselves or about their situation, they open themselves to the devil's attack.

Then Christian believers are to strap on the "breastplate of righteousness." Righteousness is presented in a twofold sense in the Scriptures. Believers are *declared* righteous in God's sight because of faith in Jesus Christ (Rom. 4:3,9). The theologians call that experience "forensic justification." But one also *becomes* righteous in Christian living by the power and work of the indwelling of the Holy Spirit. God sees his people righteous because he sees them through Jesus Christ, his Son. Moreover, he is continually making them more ethically righteous through the power of the indwelling Holy Spirit.

Look at the Christian's "new shoes." Paul says one should be shod with the "preparation of the gospel of peace" (KJV). The word *preparation* literally means "making one fully ready to plunge into the fight." The paradox in Paul's statement is quite fascinating; the preparation is for *battle*, but one is prepared with the "gospel of peace." Christians are urged to wage a war with the weapons of peace, the marvelous *peace of God*. Jesus said, "Blessed are the peacemakers, for they shall be called sons of God" (Matt. 5:9). Believers battle, but they battle with the peace of God. Yet in the final analysis, this is the only way to wage war, if one is to win for the Savior.

Then there is the ever available "shield of faith." Christians can never be secure without that defensive weapon. This has become amply evident by now.

Paul further urges believers to fit on the "helmet of salvation." Lugging that heavy steel helmet around all day seems a chore during the dreary yet strenuous hours of basic training. But when the bullets start flying, that helmet is a soldier's best friend. When one leaps out of the trenches onto the spiritual battlefield, one had best be sure that the head, the most vital part of the body, is covered in the salvation God alone can give. Simply put, if one is not saved and sure of his salvation, tremendous vulnerability to Satan's arrows is certain. And it is further certain that Satan knows exactly where to aim his fiery darts.

## A Lesson Learned

I had a most interesting experience along this line as a very young Christian. I was praying one day when suddenly a completely different "feeling" swept over me. The first thought that popped into my mind was, *I am not really saved.* I lost all my joy, assurance, and victory. My whole concern centered on whether I was truly Christian. I fought no aggressive battles and won no victories. I was completely on the defense—and losing. I did not know what to do. Then God led me to pick up a small salvation sermonette from a tract rack in a place of worship. I went through it hoping to find some help. As I came to the bottom of the page I read words to this effect: "Don't rely on your feelings; rely on God's sure promise in his Word. He cannot lie." *That's it,* I said to myself. *Feelings do not matter. What God says in the Scriptures is what counts.* I learned the great lesson of trusting God's promise alone for my assurance. Now with the helmet of salvation back firmly in place, I could wage the warfare in assurance.

Finally, Christians are to take up the "sword of the Spirit," the Word of God. This is the believer's only offensive weapon. To state the old cliché, the best defense is always an offense. Believers are never pictured in the Scriptures as standing with their backs to the wall, frantically defending the fort. Jesus said, "I will build my church, and the powers of death shall not prevail against it" (Matt. 16:18). The imagery is not that of the Christian holed up in some citadel hanging on until Jesus comes. Never! The church is to storm the stronghold of sin, Satan, and evil. The people of God are always portrayed as an offensive army. Clothed with the full armor of God, brandishing the sword of the Spirit, the church invades enemy territory and goes forth conquering in the name of Christ. Into this glorious and victorious battle we are all called. This is really revival living at its best. The revived of the Lord are more than conquerors through him who loved us. As that quality of spiritual awakening deepens and matures in our personal experience, the quality of our lives takes on the quality of Christ himself. And that is beautiful.

How beautiful are . . .
those who preach good news!
(Romans 10:15)

# 6
# The Revived Life Is a Beautiful Life

Madame Guyon, a deeply spiritual French Christian, said:

> I had a deep peace which seemed to pervade the whole soul,
> and resulted from the fact that all my desires were fulfilled in
> God. . . . I desired nothing but what I now had, because I had full
> belief that, in my present state of mind, the results of each
> moment constituted the fulfillment of the Divine purposes. . . . I
> had no will but the Divine will. One characteristic of this higher
> degree of experience was a sense of inward purity. . . . My mind
> had such a oneness with God, such a unity with the Divine
> nature, that nothing seemed to have power to soil it and to
> diminish its purity.[1]

That's beautiful. Mature saints of God always develop a
beautiful life-style. The revived life and the spiritually mature
life are identical twins. All God ever attempts to effect in any
Christian's experience is to enable one to grow into the beauty
of Jesus. Paul put it this way; "This is the will of God, even your
sanctification" (1 Thess. 4:3). J. B. Phillips translates the apostle:
"God's plan is to make you holy." God's dynamic design for our

lives is that we grow into winsome holiness and attractive consecration. God places a standard before us; our part is to grow up to meet it. The biblical, theological term for this marvelous process of maturing in consecration is "sanctification." This theme has been struck previously; now we must attack it in earnest.

## The Heart of the Matter

The essence of this significant sanctification process is found in Galatians 4:19: "Oh, my dear children, I feel the pains of childbirth all over again till Christ be formed within you" (Phillips). In this passage the pathos of Paul surges to the surface as he yearns over these early Christians, pleading that "Christ be formed within." And this yearning is but a pale reflection of how God the Father yearns over all his children. His whole work in our lives is to form Christ within. This is what sanctification is all about.

Such an in-depth work of the Holy Spirit cannot be effected overnight, however. Although Christ comes to one's life in a moment, that is just the beginning. John Wesley said, "Conversion does not get everything settled, but it gets a multitude of spiritual realities started." After being saved by Christ and receiving his glorious new life, the mind-renewing process of becoming formed into his beautiful image is inaugurated by the power of the Holy Spirit. Moreover, this process continues until the day one is made perfectly Christlike on the delightful day of resurrection. That day will dawn when Jesus comes again to take his redeemed to himself. In the meantime, revived Christians are to permit God to grow them up in Christ through the renewing of their minds (Rom. 12:1-2).

Now if believers are to be like their Lord, they must obviously bear the same fruit of holiness he did. In the end, fruit bearing is the crux of the matter. It is often said that the fruit of a Christian is another Christian. That is not exactly true. All Christians, of course, are to witness and win others to faith in their Lord. But that is the result of Spirit-directed service. The fruit of the Spirit—the quality of fruit that Christ epitomized in his character—centers in *holy living*. This principle is fully outlined in Galatians 5:22-23: "The fruit of the Spirit is love, joy, peace, patience, kindness, goodness, faithfulness, gentleness, self-control; against such there is no law." Paul pleads with God's people to permit the Holy Spirit to develop a quality of Christlike holiness in their lives through his indwelling fruit-bearing work. This is sanctification.

## Important Implications

Important implications immediately emerge from Paul's foundational passage. The Christian, as a branch grafted into the Vine, Jesus Christ, is to abide and draw life-giving sustenance from the Vine. When this abiding state is maintained, marvelous fruits are produced on these grafted branches. A look at each aspect of the Spirit-empowered, fruitful life will give insight.

## The Fruit of Love

The first beautiful fruit that blossoms with all the glory of God on Christian branches is *love*. Most significant is the fact that love is placed as the primary fruit of the Spirit. Someone has said that to put a comma after "love" in Galatians 5:24 is incorrect punctuation. A colon should be used. This implies there is really only one fruit of the Spirit: God's kind of *love*. The rest of the Galatian passage then becomes a definition or ramification of the one essential quality of love. There is a certain validity to this approach in the light of how Paul defines love in 1 Corinthians 13: "Love is patient and kind; love is not jealous or boastful; it is not arrogant or rude. Love does not insist on its own way; it is not irritable or resentful; it does not rejoice at wrong, but rejoices in the right. Love bears all things, believes all things, hopes all things, endures all things" (1 Cor. 13:4-7).

Paul's hymn to love certainly implies that the fruit of love is basic to all other Christlike graces. Still, it will prove helpful to look at each individual fruit of the Spirit presented in the Galatian passage. Every grace will reflect a fascinating facet of the foundational fruit of love.

## Joy

Joy is a beautiful blossom that sends forth its fragrance in the Christian life. The prophet Nehemiah said, "The joy of the Lord is your strength" (Nehemiah 8:10). There is nothing quite so contagious or winsomely attractive as Christian joy. Notice the prophet calls it "the joy of the Lord." It is not an earthly, temporary human joy. Christians are not happy simply because circumstances are pleasant or because they are positive-thinking people. Abiding in Christ and drawing on his life-giving strength gives a much deeper fruitage of meaning and reality to life than that. Christian joy is the deep-seated satisfaction that wells up because of the Holy Spirit and his abiding work in the heart.

Of course, believers are not always "bubbling over." Yet, it is "joy unspeakable and full of glory" (1 Pet. 1:8, KJV). The true joy of the Lord is a satisfying inner knowledge that regardless of what life hurls God is with one to meet any trial (Rom. 8:28). In that knowledge and assurance a fruit-bearing Christian rejoices.

## Peace

Faithfully abiding on the Vine and drawing on his strength will produce fruit the Bible calls "peace." Paul described it as "the peace of God, which passeth all understanding" (Phil. 4:7). Priceless, yet strangely elusive, this beautiful fruit is sought by multitudes. The fact that the shelves of book stores are lined with volumes on how to obtain inner peace verifies this. Everyone appears to be on an unbridled quest for that mysterious something called "peace of mind." People line up by the thousands for interviews with psychiatrists, hoping to find peace for troubled lives. Others try every avenue imaginable in search of this blessing. They make all the scenes human ingenuity can conjure up: pleasure, wealth, position, drugs, sex, crime, or whatever. As F. B. Meyer said, "Our natures sigh for rest, as an ocean shell, when placed to the ear, seems to cry for the untroubled depths of its native home."[2] People turn everywhere, it seems, except to the *one* source where it is to be found, in our Lord Jesus Christ. His promise is true: "Peace I leave with you; my peace I give to you; not as the world gives do I give to you. Let not your hearts be troubled, neither let them be afraid" (John 14:27).

Now notice, it is *his* peace. One does not strive for it. Nor will work produce it. It is Christ's gift to those who faithfully abide in him, and a marvelous gift it is. What is it like?

Oceanographers use the phrase, "the cushion of the sea." They tell us that below the surface of the world's great oceans there is a layer of quiet, still water. All is at rest except for the flowing of the deep ocean currents. On the surface of the seas, winds and storms whip the waters into a frenzy. But below, in the "cushion," all is calm.

So is the fruit-bearing Christian's life. Surface circumstances may blow up a serious storm. When one gets caught in the frenzy, life is anything but pleasant. Yet believers who abide in the Vine bear the peaceable fruit of contentment. They move along through the turbulent sea in the "cushion," deeply rooted and abiding in Christ. The surface may be in a fury, yet deep within there is the calm of the Spirit as the currents of his leadership move one along in the will of God. A tranquil serenity of heart prevails because of the consciousness that "our times are in the hands of God." That is peace.

Make no mistake; realism is not rejected in the quest for the peace of God. Fruit-bearing believers do not deny life's difficulties. They simply possess victory and satisfaction in the midst of situations. This is why the maturing, revived Christian can weep and have peace at the same moment. This is one more of the divine paradoxes in the experience of Christ. Only those maturing, revived, fruit-bearing believers in the Lord Jesus can understand it.

## Patience

Another fruit that bursts out on the branches that abide in the Vine is patience. One writer has defined this term as the "strength to defer anger, and the contentedness to bear injuries." The word depicts a patience in regard to *people*. Chrysostom said that patience is the quality of grace God gives to the Christian who could in justice seek revenge, but refuses to do so. The concept is constantly used concerning the Lord Jesus Christ and his attitude toward the people he encountered. If we would bear the kind of fruit that flows from Christ, patience must characterize all interpersonal relationships.

## Kindness

Kindness is another beautiful fruit that Christian branches bear. This word is akin to "goodness" and is sometimes translated that way. It implies a particular sort of goodness that is very kind. One definition expresses it as a sweetness of temper that moves us to be gracious and courteous and easy to be reconciled when we have been wronged. The word appears only in the New Testament. It is not found in secular Greek. Yet this is what the secular world sorely needs. Only the fruit-bearing Christian can display it in any real depth and thus challenge the secular scene.

## Goodness

The fruit of goodness takes its rightful place on the believer's branch. This word appears often in the Christian gospel. An interesting incident that illustrates its meaning occurred during our Lord's earthly ministry. A man came to him on an occasion and asked, "Teacher, what good deed must I do, to have eternal life?" Jesus retorted, "Why do you ask me about what is good? One there is who is good" (Matt. 19:16-17). The man asked quite a common question. The anomaly of our nature is that even though we are sinful, we are much concerned about doing and being good. Jesus put the record straight. There is only One who is good: God. He is the basis of all true goodness. So doing good and being good is to be Godlike.

On a mere human level, of course, God's quality of goodness is impossible to attain. To be good in this sense lies beyond human achievement. Yet Christians, by God's grace, bear the fruit of God's kind of goodness as they abide in Christ.

The grace of goodness is not being a "do-gooder." Rather, it denotes a "strong goodness" that God inspires. It centers in being declared righteous by God and doing righteous deeds by faith in Christ. It means, as one commentator expressed it, "Living virtuously and equipped at every point." A genuine godly attempt to be helpful to others in every phase of life is its essence. "So then, as we have opportunity, let us do good to all

men, and especially to those who are of the household of faith"
(Gal. 6:10). That is Christlikeness in the highest sense. As the
believer abides in the true Vine, he can do just that.

## Faithfulness

Faithfulness is another beautiful fruit of the Spirit that
displays a manifestation of God's love. This term is the common
word for "trustworthiness." It denotes a person who is totally
reliable, just as God is. Honesty and justice and fidelity in what
one professes and promises is implied. It is active; it grows out
of love and vibrant faith in God. Of course, faithfulness to God
will obviously make one trustworthy to others.

## Gentleness

With faithfulness as a basic stance before God, a proper
attitude and relationship to people becomes the next lovely fruit
of the Spirit to bloom on the branch; the Bible calls it "gentleness." This beautiful fruit shines forth the glory of the Vine,
Jesus Christ, for he was such a man. Jesus said, "I am gentle
and lowly in heart" (Matt. 11:29). He further stated, "Blessed are
the meek, for they shall inherit the earth" (Matt. 5:5). This grace
is threefold. In the first place it signifies a submission to the will
of God (Matt. 11:29). It further means that a gentle Christian is
teachable, one who is not too proud to learn (Jas. 1:21). Finally,
it exalts the spirit and attitude of consideration (1 Cor. 4:21). The
adjectival form of the word refers to an animal that has been
trained and brought under control. For the fruit-bearing Christian it signifies that when one is wronged, there is no display of
resentment or vengeance. The exact opposites of gentleness are
arrogance, vehemence, bitterness, wildness, and violence. Of
course, our Lord never exhibited any of these attitudes. Meek-

ness is not weakness; Jesus was anything but a weak man. Gentleness and meekness are strength.

## Self-Control

The final fruit that blossoms on the Christian branch because of constant abiding in the Vine is termed "self-control." The philosopher Plato used this word to convey the concept of self-mastery. It applies to the person who has mastered all his desires and his love of pleasure. Paul employed the term in relationship to an athlete's discipline of his body (1 Cor. 9:25) and to the Christian's mastery of sex (1 Cor. 7:9). Strength of character is at the heart of the idea. Thus it is possible for Christians so to master themselves that they are able to be the right kind of self-giving servants to others.

## A Big Order

That is what it is like to be a fruit-bearing branch. A beautiful life to be sure—love in the highest sense of the word! But it is an almost unbelievable order. Is it really attainable?

The demand is before every revived believer. But how can one bear such a beautiful cluster of fruit? In answer, another question is pertinent: How does a typical branch, say of a grapevine, bear fruit? By struggling to do so? Of course not! It just abides in the vine. When it does, the life-giving sap flows into it. The branch quite naturally bears grapes because it is properly attached to the vine and lives off the vine's life-giving sustenance. That is its design.

The solution to our inadequacy immediately emerges. When we as branches abide in the Vine, Jesus Christ, his own life-giving power in the person of the Holy Spirit flows into us, and we just naturally bear fruit. There is no struggle in bearing fruit; it occurs simply because the Holy Spirit is within and his power flows through us. In the final analysis, it is his fruit, not ours. There is a struggle, but it is not a battle to bear fruit by human determination. The effort is to let Christ's life be formed within and then lived out. That is a struggle of faith. Thus, we are back to the basic principle of faith in Christian experience.

In the entire fruit-bearing process, it is vital to realize that Christ *himself* is formed in the personhood of the believer by the power of the Holy Spirit (Gal. 4:19). Christian consecration is not mimicking Jesus. Christ's own life is actually formed within and expressed through the surrendered, abiding child of God. Strictly speaking, we Christians are never to be an *imitation* of Christ. Attempting to imitate Jesus in one's own strength can soon degenerate into legalism if not outright humanism. Rather, we are to be an *embodiment* of our lovely Lord. In that way alone God can glorify himself, because only in that manner does the Christian reflect his Son and hence bear his fruit. In simplest terms, we live the exchanged life, the Christ life for the self-life.

## The Exchanged Life

Notice, a so-called "good Christian life" is not exchanged for the *self*-life. It is *Christ's own fruitful life* we receive. Oswald Chambers put the principle this way: " . . . all that Christ wrought *for* me on the Cross is wrought *in* me. The free committal of myself to God gives the Holy Spirit the chance to impart to me the holiness of Jesus Christ."[3]

Striving in one's own strength to be a good Christian is to cling to the old self-life in an attempt to make it like Jesus. It won't work. The self-life, the unrenewed mind, can never be transformed. It must be put to death by faith just like any other manifestation of the old life. As already made clear, it is Christ's own life manifest through us by our identification with him in death and resurrection. In that way, and in that way alone, are we truly Christlike, because Jesus himself lives through us and hence bears his fruit. As one author expressed it, "Christian living is not our living with Christ's help, it is Christ living his life in us. Therefore, that portion of our lives that is not his living is not Christian living, and that portion of our service that is not his doing is not Christian service; for all such life and service have but a human and natural source, and Christian life and service have a supernatural and spiritual source."[4] Paul said, "For me to live is Christ" (Phil. 1:21).

The primary principle of the exchanged life is "rest," a rest of faith. Martin Luther said, "Therefore, we must nestle under the wings of this mother hen, and not rashly fly away trusting in the powers of our own faith, lest the hawk speedily tear us in pieces and devour us." That is the secret: staying on the ground of a surrendered faith, continually walking with Christ, and letting his life of beauty and power and fruit-bearing be lived through us. Thus we grow into a beautiful manifestation of Christ that brings honor and glory to God who redeemed us. A revived life is a beautiful life.

Does this resting mean we do not serve God with zeal? Emphatically not! We will serve our Lord Jesus Christ as never before. But the quality will be different, so different. Living the Spirit-filled, awakened life does not imply that one turns in on one's self and just concentrates on how to be blessed personally. Never! That is a pitfall to be avoided *at all costs*. A real awakened Christian will serve. There are needs all around. A world cries out for Christ and salvation. Real revived believers answer that call. To that final aspect of personal revival we turn.

> Therefore, my beloved brethren, be steadfast, immovable, always abounding in the work of the Lord, knowing that in the Lord your labor is not in vain. (1 Corinthians 15:58)

# 7
# The Revived Life Is a Contributing Life

One of the most magnificent works of faith in recent Christian times was epitomized in the ministry of George Muller of Bristol, England. His efforts were tireless as he cared for thousands of orphans in needy Britain in the 1800s. Remember, it was this great work that first moved D. L. Moody to travel to England. The Muller saga is one of the most beautiful stories of faith one can read. What a contributing life he lived!

Muller began his labors in Bristol in 1832. At that time, he served as a copastor with his fellow minister Mr. Craik at Gideon and Bethesda Chapels. The membership of the churches quadrupled in a very short time, and that was all by faith; neither man received a salary. Muller continued to preach in Bristol even after he began his orphanage work. At the time of his death, he had a congregation of two thousand persons at Bethesda Chapel.

In 1834, Mr. Muller founded the Scripture Knowledge Institution for Home and Abroad. This work went on through Muller's life. By the time of his death, 122,000 persons had been taught in schools supported by his efforts; 282,000 Bibles and 1,500,000 Testaments had been distributed; also 112,000,000 religious books, pamphlets, and tracts had been circulated; and missionaries had been aided all over the globe.

When Muller became seventy years old, he began to make evangelistic tours. During this time he traveled two hundred thousand miles, going around the world. He preached in many countries and in several different languages. Three times he preached throughout the United States. He continued his evangelistic ministry to the age of ninety years. During these years of evangelistic work he spoke to three million people. Moreover, all his expenses were met in answer to the prayer of faith.

Yet, all agree that of all of Muller's undertakings, the orphanages of Bristol were the greatest work of faith. He began that with only two shillings (20 cents), but, being a man of great faith and prayer, he received the funds necessary to build buildings, feed and clothe orphans, and meet the needs of thousands for sixty years. Muller never asked for one penny. Yet, in all that time the children never missed a meal. Muller said that if they ever had to go without a meal he would take it as evidence that the Lord did not want the work to continue.

Muller learned early that to trust the Lord for a shilling was as difficult as to trust him for a thousand pounds ($2,000). But trust he did. Funds for one project after another were received in answer to prayer. Six hundred pounds a week were required for the support of the orphans at the time of Muller's death. And the Lord sent it in day by day.

The inspiration for Muller's work came when he saw the orphanage at Halle, in Prussia. In Bristol, Muller felt that the Lord was leading him to begin a similar work. He wanted to give a testimony to the world that the Lord still hears and answers prayer. God met that step of faith; Muller will always be remembered for his great work of faith and prayer. After his task was done, the Lord gently removed him. He went to his reward on the night of March 10, 1898.

The George Muller story reveals to us some vital realities about the awakened life. Two climactic characteristics, as Muller demonstrated, inevitably lead to the summit of any revival mountain: (1) God's people begin serving with zest and effectiveness; and (2) the revived develop a fervent prayer life. In a word, God revives the redeemed to make them contributing Christians.

The Bible bursts with examples—even commands—that revived people serve Christ and help others. Several reasons are found for this fact.

## Serving the World's Needs

In the first place, Christian service is important for the sake of our desperate world. Our Lord said Christians are to be "the salt of the earth" (Matt. 5:13). As salt flavors, purifies, and preserves, the Christian is to exemplify similar spiritual qualities. Christ expects his people to permeate society with a flavoring, purifying, preserving influence.

Something of a *flavoring quality* should constantly radiate from the child of God. How? D. L. Moody, the nineteenth-century evangelist, was preaching to a great congregation in a large hall. On the wall of the hall hung a huge billboard with the text: "God is love" (1 John 4:8). Moody pointed to the sign and said, "God is love! I believe that in any great city, thousands would be converted if they only believed the truth that 'God is love.'"

Moody was right. If people could only grasp how Christ loves them, they would surely be moved to the Lord. But how will they believe? What will bring them to this knowledge? Perhaps a few will be reached by reading posters and roadside signs to that effect. This may get the message across to some. But not too many will believe by merely reading. What about preaching? Will this convert the world? Hardly! True, there are those who hear the preaching of God's love and believe. That is obvious. But there are millions more who never come near a church or turn on a religious program or go to a rally where the love of God is forthrightly proclaimed. What about them?

There is only one way by which the mass of humanity will come to know and understand that God is love and hence be moved to our loving Lord. It will happen when God's own people themselves are filled to overflowing with the love of Christ and engage in sacrificial acts of love. Then, and then alone, will the world as a whole understand the glorious truth of God's compassion. In a word, the world needs to see a *living demonstration* that God is love. This is one of the primary principles of being the salt of the earth. When God's people are revived by the Holy Spirit and transformed into people of loving service, they flavor their entire sphere of influence with the love of Christ. That is what it means to be the salt of the earth. But do not forget Jesus' warning, "If the salt has lost its taste. . . . It is no longer good for anything except to be thrown out and trodden under foot by men" (Matt. 5:13).

Salt also has a *purifying quality*. That characteristic should mark the Christian life. Previously, mention was made of Bertha Smith. She exemplifies in a beautiful manner the purifying quality of salt. Few can ever be the same after having been in fellowship with Bertha. I am a better Christian because I have met her and fallen under her influence. When they are revived, Christians purify others by the purity and beauty of their own fruit-bearing lives. That is being the salt of the earth, too.

Finally, *salt preserves*. The church in its universal and institutional aspects demonstrates this reality. How different communities are because of the influence of the church! Schools, hospitals, children's homes, and a multitude of other great benevolent movements found their inception in the revived church. For example, during the great prayer awakening in the middle of the last century, over six hundred American Christian colleges were instituted by revived evangelicals. Nothing preserves society like the revived church.

The principle of preservation can be clearly seen on an individual basis also. The vital service of personal witnessing for Christ, for instance, enables a Christian to become the "salt of the earth." In sharing the good news of the Lord Jesus with others, and leading them to personal faith and commitment to Christ, people are "preserved" to eternal life.

An illustration of what one man can accomplish as a personal witness is the story of M. L. O'Neal. This man was the most effective witness for Jesus Christ I have ever personally known. He was the "salt of the earth" with a preserving quality like few Christians ever possess. He was not a pastor; he served the Lord as a layman. He was not highly educated. In his early days he had to drop out of school and go to work on the small Texas farm on which he was raised. Later in life, he moved to Fort Worth and through hard work became a very successful business man. From a small beginning, his business as a housebuilder grew until he had constructed thousands of dwellings for people.

The fact that a poor farm boy moved to the big city and made good is not the real heart of his story, however. His most remarkable quality lay in his ability to lead others to faith in Jesus Christ. He was actually something of a genius in sharing his faith. He had an ardent passion to win the unconverted such as is seldom seen. He seized every opportunity to witness for Christ. In every conceivable context a word would be shared. He would witness to waitresses in restaurants, attendants at filling stations, clerks in stores—wherever he met people. His whole life was built around this one goal. I remember his driving thousands of miles to share Christ. As his pastor, I have been with him scores of times as we visited homes. Often whole families would be brought to faith by his effective witness.

Brother O'Neal, as we affectionately called him, was not a great Bible scholar, though he faithfully read his Bible. He was anything but a theologian. His speaking ability was not outstanding. He rarely spoke publicly. He never held any important leadership position in his church. But he was so full of the Holy Spirit that just a few words seemed to bring people under conviction of sin. At the same time, he was so skillful he rarely offended anyone. I know for a fact that he led literally hundreds to faith in the Lord Jesus Christ. In reality, he burned out his life seeking others for the Savior.

He became seriously ill some time ago. An operation was mandatory. As he was being prepared for surgery, he faithfully witnessed to the male nurse who was caring for him. Although he survived the actual surgery, he died a short time later. His last real intelligent conversation on earth was an attempt to win someone else to faith in Christ. What a way to go! His whole life was consumed with this one passion. One of the most difficult things I ever had to do as a pastor was to preach at his funeral. I felt as if I had lost a spiritual father as well as a brother. But as I looked over the large congregation that gathered in the church, I could see many he had won to Christ. What a triumph!

I realize that few of us will ever become as effective in witnessing as Brother O'Neal. But all can be as committed, and many of us could do far more than we are now attempting. We are all to be the salt of the earth; we ought to be about the work of "preserving." Remember, if salt loses its taste, it is good for nothing.

This reeling world desperately needs the ministry of Christians. It will never be flavored, purified, or preserved unless revived believers take their rightful stance and salt it.

## Serving to Glorify God

Moreover, sincere service glorifies God. Seeking his glory is always to be the Christian's utmost motive. When Paul entered Athens and saw their idolatry, their ignorance, and disregard for the knowledge of the true God, "his spirit was provoked within him as he saw that the city was full of idols" (Acts 17:16). Divine jealousy stirred the apostle. He was deeply moved with emotion that the name of Jesus should be honored by all. As John Stott put it, "He burned with longing that the Athenians should know and honor the God they either ignorantly worshiped or actually by their idolatry denied."[1] So Paul courageously declared Christ in the marketplace or wherever anyone would listen. God's honor was at stake. The Shorter Catechism correctly expresses it: "Man's chief end is to glorify God, and to enjoy him for ever." The whole purpose for living is to magnify the name of Jesus Christ. That is why we serve. That is why we live.

## Serving to Further the Kingdom

We are taught to pray,

> Our Father who art in heaven,
> Hallowed be thy name.
> Thy kingdom come,
> Thy will be done,
>     On earth as it is in heaven. (Matt. 6:9-10)

By our properly motivated service, we actually further God's kingdom. In a sense, we can be a partial answer to our own prayers. That is life at its best. That brings real purpose and meaning into each day. That is revived living at its height.

Surely all true believers at least attempt to serve Christ in some way. At the same time, however, most of us have had some rather frustrating experiences in Christian service. Why? Why do our feverish efforts so often seem to accomplish so little?

Perhaps the reason for seeming failure in much Christian service is because of the attempt to serve God and extend the kingdom in a way the Holy Spirit does not direct. If such be the case, one can hardly expect God's blessings or the Spirit's power. God's work must be done in God's way. Activity alone is not enough. How then can one be assured of serving Christ according to God's plan?

## Serving God His Way

Approaching this vital theme, it must first be recognized that all Christians make up what the Bible calls the ministering "body of Christ." There are many figures in the New Testament to describe the people of God. The church is variously pictured as the bride of Christ, God's vineyard, God's flock, God's building, a holy priesthood, the new Israel, and a holy nation. Perhaps the most graphic is to view the church as a *body*. It seems to be the favorite of Paul. The figure is apt, especially regarding Christian service. What does a "body" do? It moves, functions, and acts—it works. Scripturally, the serving church always ministers as a functioning *body* of Christ. This approach to the service of the church has two important implications.

## Some Important Implications

First, as a body has different parts with different functions, so does a local church in its ministry. To say all members of a congregation are the same and therefore are to do the same thing in service is not realistic. Abilities, gifts, talents, and ministries vary with each member. Paul asked, "Are all apostles? Are all prophets? Are all teachers? Do all work miracles? Do all possess gifts of healing? Do all speak in tongues? Do all interpret?" (1 Cor. 12:29-30). "For just as the body is one and has many members, and all the members of the body, though many, are one body, so it is with Christ. For by one Spirit we were all baptized into one body" (1 Cor. 12:12-13). There is a diversity of members and corresponding functions at a local church level, just as a body has a diversity of members with corresponding functions. This must be recognized if a church is to be a true, serving body of Christ.

Second, the metaphor of the body further suggests that in the church's diversity there still remains a central, inescapable unity. In a sense, a body is always a single unit. This means, as far as the church is concerned, that all the members stand equal and one before God. It is the one Holy Spirit that enables all Christians to say, "Jesus is Lord." Moreover, as the body is a whole, so also is the basic responsibility in Christian ministry. That is, the commission to serve God was given to the entire body. John Stott reminds us, "The essential unity of the Church, originating in the call of God and illustrated in the metaphors of the Scripture, lead us to this conclusion: the responsibilities which God has entrusted to His Church He has entrusted to His *Whole Church*."[2] In other words, *every* Christian is to serve God as a member of the body of Christ. God allows no exemptions. There are to be no lame legs or withered arms in Christ's body. The church as a diversified yet unified body fulfills its purpose only when every member gives of himself unreservedly to worship and service.

This raises another important query: What relationship is implied between the so-called laity and clergy in the body metaphor? Answer: the laity are the whole people of God, and the clergy are given the privilege of oversight, shepherding, and equipping them for service. Paul brings this out very clearly in Ephesians 4:11-12: "And his gifts were that some should be apostles, some prophets, some evangelists, some pastors and teachers, to equip the saints for the work of ministry, for building up the body of Christ."

Many illustrations have been presented to demonstrate Paul's principle. Elton Trueblood, for example, likens the clergyman to the coach of a football team. The coach's responsibility is to instruct, teach, motivate, and direct the play. The team, on the other hand, has the major role in actually playing the game. The minister is the coach, and the entire team, the laity, plays the game. Or perhaps one can visualize the minister as a filling-station attendant. The layman gets his car "filled up" with fuel and kept in repair by the man at the station. But it is the layman who does the actual running of the car, not the attendant or the mechanic.

Of course, the minister is a part of the people of God also. By virtue of that fact, he also "plays the game" and "drives the car." But that is essentially because he is a Christian, not because he is a clergyman. In a word, he is the helper and equipper of the layman so that the layman can get on with the job, not *vice versa*. As John Stott pointed out, if anyone belongs to anybody in the church, it is not the laity who belong to the clergy, but the clergy who belong to the laity. With this relationship in the diversified but integrated body, the work of Christ can go forward effectively.

## The Key Question

Therefore, the key question becomes: How can a church be organized so as to become a healthy, virile, fully functioning body of Christ to serve the world? Several passages in the writings of Paul answer the question forthrightly. In Ephesians 4, Romans 12, and 1 Corinthians 12, Paul emphatically states that the church becomes the servant church on the basis of the bestowal of spiritual, ministering gifts. That is, God equips the church for ministry with special endowments called the gifts of the Spirit. These grace gifts enable the church to serve Christ with power and effect.

This theme must be confronted cautiously, however. Much misunderstanding revolves around the idea of the gifts of the Spirit. The biblical concept is often seriously misinterpreted today. Perversions of the teaching of the Scriptures on this theme have hurt many churches. Furthermore, when one addresses this theme, there is always the danger of being "labeled." So we must tread softly on this road. Yet we forthrightly approach the Word of God and hear what it has to say.

Perhaps the single most important fact to realize is that the gifts of the Spirit are given to the church *for ministry*. They are not bestowed for personal, spiritual indulgence of any kind. The Holy Spirit graciously imparts these gifts so that believers may be effective in their service for the Savior. If this principle is kept constantly in mind, many errors can be sidestepped and the emotions defused. God simply gives spiritual gifts so Christians can serve Christ with effect. That is the primary purpose. Now to the biblical basis of this concept.

## What the Bible Says

This teaching had significant prominence in the life of the early church. This is obvious because of the lengthy passages, already referred to, found in the Pauline body of literature. From these prominent passages a series of vital principles come forward and cry to be heard.

Paul states that when Christ ascended back to the Father, He "led a host of captives,/and he gave gifts to men" (Ephesians 4:8). These "gifts" are the consequence of the presence of the

"Spirit of promise." It is important to distinguish these gifts of the Spirit from the fruit of the Spirit discussed earlier. The fruit is the manifestations of the Spirit in daily life to develop Christlike character. The gifts are the manifestation of the Holy Spirit through the believer to make service effectual. This fact becomes very evident in the listing of the gifts of the Spirit enumerated in the three primary passages mentioned above. First Corinthians 12:8-10 lists the following:

1. utterance of wisdom;
2. utterance of knowledge;
3. faith;
4. healing;
5. miracles;
6. prophecies;
7. discernment of spirits;
8. various kinds of tongues;
9. interpretation of tongues.

In 1 Corinthians 12:28-29, the following are listed:

1. apostles;
2. prophets;
3. teachers;
4. workers of miracles;
5. healers;
6. helpers;
7. administrators;
8. speakers in various kinds of tongues.

Romans 12:6-8 presents additions to the Corinthian passage:

1. prophecy;
2. service;
3. teaching;
4. exhortation;
5. giving;
6. aiding;
7. mercy.

Eliminating the obvious duplications in Paul's passages, nineteen gifts are recorded. From this number, it becomes quite evident that the entire work of the ministry of Christian service is met in these spiritual gifts. This is why Paul stressed their significance and says, "Now concerning spiritual gifts, brethren, I do not want you to be uninformed" (1 Cor. 12:1). What can now be said in more detail about this central theme?

## Details Discussed

It becomes clear initially that some gifts lay stress on Christian personalities who themselves have particular ministries, for example, apostles, prophets, teachers. In other instances, the emphasis rests upon the function rather than on the individual who is gifted, for example, faith and varieties of tongues. Yet this distinction should not be pressed too far. Probably the simplest thing to say is that a gift apart from a believer to exercise the gift is meaningless, and a Christian who is not exercising his gift is a relatively ineffectual servant of Christ. The gift and the gifted weave the warp and woof of the fabric. You cannot have the one without the other.

Second, the gifts of the Spirit are not to be confused with natural talents. Though all people have some natural abilities, abilities that God will surely use in his service, the spiritual gifts are not talents *per se*. One commentator has pointed this out by stating that the believers were endowed "with certain powers which they had not previously possessed and which were due to the influence of the Holy Spirit."[3] Spiritual gifts are *grace* gifts of the Holy Spirit. He alone is the author. Christians do not assume them of their own volition. They are *supernatural* endowments. Yet the distinction between gifts and talents should not be pushed to an extreme conclusion. This would tend to imply that it is gifts *alone* that God uses and not our natural abilities. In the actual practice of Christian ministry, they probably just blend in with one another; thus, in the personality of the gifted and talented believer God glorifies himself.

Third, the gifts should be exercised only under the control of the Holy Spirit. Paul is most emphatic about this. They are not to be employed simply when and how the believer wishes, let alone selfishly enjoyed. "The operator . . . is always God; every one of the gifts in every person that manifests them . . . is bestowed and set in motion by him."[4] On this point we must practice precision. Paul obviously wrote the lengthy passage in 1 Corinthians 12-14 to direct the use of the gifts under the Holy Spirit. The Corinthian believers were apparently making some serious mistakes. The apostle's attempt was to save the church from abuses and to place the entire employment of the gifts into the hands of the sovereign God.

Fourth, it is vital that all believers come alive to the fact that they have at least one or more spiritual endowments. Paul said, "But grace was given to each of us according to the measure of Christ's gift" (Eph. 4:7). Make no mistake here; all true Christians are gifted believers. To say you have no ministering gift is tantamount to saying you are not even in the body of Christ. The practical outcome of this fact is simple; you can and hence should serve Jesus Christ. The Holy Spirit abides within, not only to lead and direct and empower, but to enable the Christian by his gifts to serve Jesus Christ faithfully and effectively.

To summarize, the gifts are to be understood as Spirit-imparted grace gifts, God-given abilities to serve, divine manifestations of the Holy Spirit through believers for the enrichment of the body and for the development of the work of the ministry in Christian service. As one expressed it, "It is simply the Holy Spirit working through us in a given manner, at a given time he, the Spirit, chooses, for carrying out the ministry to which we have been appointed of God."[5] This "carrying out the ministry" is a vitally important aspect of the overall theme. What actually happens when the gifts are in operation?

## The Pragmatics

The following delineation of the outworking of the spiritual gifts should help.

1. For the proclamation of God's self-disclosure: the gift of prophecy or preaching. This is to proclaim God's truth so as to exhort, comfort, and help people.

2. For teaching the divine revelation: the gift of teaching.

3. For enabling God's blessing to flow into needy lives: the gift of faith that enables believers to rest upon God's promises and trust in the power that is beyond the sphere of human possibilities.

4. For the revelation of God's will and purpose in matters: the gift of wisdom so that God's purpose in his Word may be grasped.

5. For understanding the practical application of eternal principles in daily experience: the utterance of knowledge.

6. For protection against evil: the gift of discernment of spirits.

7. For the practical manifestation of the love of Christ, three gifts: mercy, the Paraclete gift, and giving.

8. For maintaining order in the life and work of the church: the gift of government. This gift stresses the importance of church administration.

9. For help in the community: the gift of serviceable ministries or "helps."

10. As special signs of God's power and presence, four gifts: miracles, healings, tongues, and interpretations of tongues.[6]

Some important points come to the fore in this brief outline. First, and obviously, the number of gifts found in the Scriptures is comparatively small—only nineteen. This forces one to the conclusion that each gift should be understood as a designation of a *class* of gifts. In each classification there will no doubt be many variations. Circumstances, situations, and needs vary from culture to culture and from generation to generation, hence, the need for variety under differing conditions. These biblical gifts must be understood as flexible in their outworking so as to meet the relevant needs of all people at all times.

Second, although the lists in the Bible may seem relatively short, it is also clear that the Spirit still makes full provision for all the needs of the church in its growth, worship, and worldwide ministry. The organization of the local church, its government, its instruction and equipping, its worship, its ministry of witness, and its entire corporate life are fully provided for. The Holy Spirit will surely see to it that no part of his work suffers for lack of a gift if the church is open to his leadership and ready to receive all he has to give.

Third, the principle of spiritual gifts is what makes the local church a true body of Christ. The Holy Spirit bestows the gifts "as he wills" (1 Cor. 12:11). Thus, he will never create a body that is not fully developed and functional. To build a body that is all hands or eyes or feet is a bit ludicrous. The Holy Spirit will always construct a perfectly functioning and unified organism. Therefore, it is somewhat ridiculous to think that all believers should possess the same gift. It would never be a body of Christ at all if such were the case. The Spirit creates a body that is healthy and well proportioned.

Finally, when gifted church members employ their ministry under the direction of the Holy Spirit, the church is built up and strengthened, and the work of the kingdom progresses. As William Barclay states, "The picture we get is the picture of a Church vividly alive. Things happened; in fact astonishing things happened. Life was heightened and intensified and sensitised. There was nothing flat and dull and ordinary about the early Church."[7]

## Essential Conclusions

In the light of all that has been said concerning spiritual gifts, here is what seems essential to know and do. In the first place, the church should be organized so that the members of the body can exercise their gifts. It may well be that in most congregations this is already accomplished to a greater or lesser degree *implicitly*. What is called for, however, is an *explicit* structuring of the organizational pattern of the local church along the lines of spiritual gifts. The church's program should be developed in such a manner that the Holy Spirit can manifest himself in and through his people as he wills. The church must develop itself as a people-centered organism, not simply a program-oriented organization. This obviously calls for a number of revolutionary approaches. To move from a program-centered organizational structure to a people-need approach is no small undertaking. Yet undertake it we must if we would be scriptural in our church-ministry life.

Furthermore, if we take seriously the lay-centered ministry concept and believe that God's Spirit empowers and gives gifts to *all* Christians, we must expect *all of God's people* to get on with their respective responsibilities. After all, is not the priesthood of all believers predicated on this principle? Such an approach to Christian service is very practical; it saves one from feeling inadequate for the task and thus inspires responsibility in Christ's service. We have been gifted by the Holy Spirit. We *can* do what God desires. We have a gift from God to exercise. We can thus expect God's power and blessings and leadership in the exercise of that gift. Service can be genuine, meaningful, and effective in bringing glory to Jesus Christ. The lay people must be liberated to exercise their gifts. Church planners must desist from cramming folks into molds.

## How to Discover Your Gift

The question now becomes: How can Christians know what gifts they possess? It should first be understood that there is no presumption in saying one has a gift. No one earned them or worked for them; nor were they bestowed because of some special merit. They were given to all solely by the grace of the Spirit in accordance with his will. The glory belongs to God who grants his gifts for his honor and praise. Now to the issue of discovering one's own gift.

Guiding principles can be discovered from the Scriptures and experience. The following are some of the basic spiritual disciplines in discovering one's ministry; I call them the "Ten Commandments of Discovering Your Spiritual Gifts."

1. Have confidence you have one, or more. The Bible says you do.

2. Study the Scriptures; they have the answers to questions on the theme.

3. Ask: How has God used me in the past, *really* used me? That may give some clues.

4. Ask: What do spiritual people say? They may provide some clues. Others often understand us better than we do ourselves. Sharing can be most important.

5. Ask: What do I like to do? We like to do what we do well. We should do well in the exercising of our gift.

6. Ask: What needs burden me? God may want me to do that service.

7. Ask: What challenges me; that is, what does the Holy Spirit lay on my heart?

8. Ask: What open doors are before me? What opportunities are present? God may be in it.

9. Rest in Jesus.
    *a.* Do something—keep moving—be disciplined.
    *b.* Be open to change.
10. Prayer and trust in God's leadership must be relied upon.

Today there are pressing needs all about. People everywhere are desperately reaching out for help, every kind of help. If we are Christians and want to live a revived life-style, we have a solemn responsibility before God to step in and meet those needs. And God has graciously equipped us to do just that. If a personal revival means anything, it means getting on with the task of serving our Lord Jesus Christ. The revived life is a serving life.

## The Centrality of Prayer for Personal Revival

Overt service is not enough for the revived Christian, however. There is another essential aspect to the revived, ministering life. The second vital contribution of the believer to meet world needs centers in prayer, intercession for a desperate day. The world waits to be moved to God, and that divine impact comes only by sacrificial, unusual prayer. The "divine mix" that always ferments revival is a desperate need, a willing God who is providentially maneuvering circumstances to a climax, and a dedicated handful of prevailing prayer warriors who will intercede until the revival dawns. In a word, a spiritual praying band and the sovereignty of God form the warp and woof of awakenings. That recipe always provides bread for the hungry.

I have become absolutely convinced that lack of prayer is the only reason revival on a grand scale has not yet come. Unless we add that leaven in our spiritual lump, the recipe for revival is ruined and the bread for the hungry will never rise. Prayer is the channel through which all personal and worldwide awakenings flow. This can be seen over and again. Bernard of Clairvaux spent months in seclusion every year seeking God.

Then he moved out on a six-months preaching mission that rocked every city he entered. Martin Luther expended hours and hours in prayer. David Brainerd agonized on his knees in deep snow, coughing blood from tubercular lungs, soaking wet with perspiration, as he interceded for the American Indians. Missionary John "Praying" Hyde, mentioned earlier, poured out his soul sacrificially for revival in India.

In John Wesley's London home, I have stood in a tiny room with its single kneeling bench where Wesley spent the early hours every day interceding for the English awakening. I was so moved as I recalled the events of those great days of revival that I could not help falling on my knees on that old kneeling bench and asking God to do it again. What is it going to take for it to happen in our time? The answer is so simple: no prayer—no revival; much prayer—much blessings. Samuel Chadwick expressed it correctly:

> There is no power like that of prevailing prayer—of Abraham pleading for Sodom, Jacob wrestling in the stillness of the night, Moses standing in the breach, Hannah intoxicated with sorrow, David heartbroken with remorse and grief, Jesus in sweat of blood. Add to this list from the records of the church your personal observation and experience, and always there is the cost of passion unto blood. Such prayer prevails. It turns ordinary mortals into men of power. It brings power. It brings fire. It brings rain. It brings life. It brings God.[8]

Matthew Henry said, "When God is ready to pour out unusual mercies, He sets His people a-praying." And I might add, *unusual* praying.

How are we to engage in that kind and quality of prayer? What does the Holy Spirit precipitate in revived lives when he sets his people "a-praying" in such an unusual way that revivals erupt? This must be learned. In a very real sense, all that has been presented up to this point in the entirety of this book is to move us to this present inquiry. If the Holy Spirit has in any sense and in any way touched your life and revived you, then let him set you "a-praying" for a deep and profound spiritual awakening. But we must learn to intercede in God's way.

## Praying Correctly

Prayer must be exercised "according to the rules," if we are to expect answers. The Bible tells us what these "rules" are. Moreover, the Holy Spirit will guide one into these realities. He has been called the "Teacher" in the "school of prayer." He deeply desires to instruct revived people in effectual prayer.

Be very clear that when one speaks about "rules" of prayer, it by no means implies that prayer is an inflexible, legalistic, wooden framework of spiritual exercise. If there is any experience in the Christian life where real liberty is found, it is in prayer. In the final analysis, prayer is just conversing with God. It is a divine-human dialogue. Prayer is no more than simply letting Jesus into one's life to meet needs. To liken the Holy Spirit to a teacher in the art of prayer is never meant to picture him as a stern school principal who is ready to apply the rod if ever in the course of any prayer experience one does not pray exactly according to plan. "Where the Spirit of the Lord is, there is freedom" (2 Cor. 3:17). The Father is amazingly understanding. He looks down into the very heart of our personhood, and when he finds sincerity and genuine longings he is well pleased. Therefore, one must never get so preoccupied with the forms and patterns and laws of prayer that a simple look to a loving Father and a pouring out of the deepest desires of the heart are somehow missed.

At the same time, however, there are at least "guidelines" that the Bible sets forth to lead one into meaningful prayer experi-

ences. We should acquaint ourselves with these. They will aid
our prayers to be purposeful and in line with what the Holy
Spirit attempts to teach us as he guides us into a rich and
deeper prayer life. Therefore, initially look at the principle of
*praying constantly.*

## Praying Without Ceasing

Paul urged all believers to "Pray without ceasing" (1 Thess.
5:17). Let's imagine a dialogue with Paul. What do you mean by
this challenge, Paul? He answers, "First of all, God expects us to
have a regular, consistent, disciplined, dedicated prayer life. All
have daily needs. Therefore, a prayer time should become a
daily spiritual habit, as God wills and permits." Paul would
further have us know that the specific time is not important nor
is some particular posture of the body vital. A Christian can
pray at any hour or in any physical position as long as sincerity
and humility are foremost in seeking God's presence. The fact
that one gives time for prayer and then sincerely intercedes are
the essential ingredients.

Some years ago I learned a vital lesson on the point of
physical aspects in prayer. We are often told we must always
pray on our knees with closed eyes. Yet when I prayed in that
posture, I had trouble keeping my mind on the subject of my
prayers. I would be praying for someone or some situation and
suddenly find my thoughts wandering off in a thousand
different directions. Many have this trouble. One day I was
reading a book on prayer, and the author confessed he had
faced a similar quandary. He shared how he had learned to
pray with concentration by walking around the room with his
eyes open while he conversed with God. That struck a respon-
sive chord. I tried it. It worked. Now in my times of prayer with
the Lord Jesus Christ, I walk about with my eyes open. It helps

tremendously, and my prayer life has been deepened significantly.

Another implication of Paul's statement to the Thessalonian church came home to me on an occasion. I visited in the home of some Christian friends several years ago. Over the kitchen sink was a motto which read, "Divine services are conducted here daily." That really is a sublime thought. We are able to pray in all our daily pursuits. Whether we are washing the dishes, working on the job, or merely walking down the street, we are challenged constantly to cast our thoughts Godward in prayer. The Lord Jesus Christ *always* has his ear open to our prayer. We need not go through some series of religious exercises to bring our needs and desires to God. Moment by moment we can lift our hearts to his very presence. Such a privilege is a rich source of blessings to the person who will constantly pray in such a manner. We should live in an attitude of prayer so that at any moment we will call on our gracious Heavenly Father and be assured he will hear. Paul, you said a lot in your little three-word phrase, "Pray without ceasing." "Yes," Paul might answer, "And that is where it all begins." But there is more.

## Pray Specifically

A further principle of effective praying centers in the problem that prayer is often made in such nebulous terms that nothing is actually requested. Simply to ask God to meet needs or to bless in a general way is not to ask for the actual things needed. The Bible urges us to get to the *real issues*. If you need wisdom to make a decision, ask God for that specifically. If you need to be revived, ask for that. Spiritual prayer principles do not exclude physical needs either. If you need a new coat, ask for a new coat. Christians who pray in this manner find that in seeking specific things, far more answers to prayer are forthcoming.

And, quite naturally, this principle applies to praise. We should praise, bless, and thank the Lord for all his goodness. He is most worthy of our praise.

## Praying in God's Will

Jesus was agonizing in the garden of Gethsemane. He ended his earnest petition with a phrase, "Yet it must not be what I want, but what you want" (Matt. 26:39, Phillips). We too must ask for things that are *in the will of God*. Only then can we expect God to answer. John tells us that "We can approach God with confidence for this reason: if we make requests which accord with his will he listens to us" (1 John 5:14, NEB). Real prayer is born when that prayer is offered according to God's will.

The question therefore becomes: How can one know the will of God in prayer? First, reading the Bible is essential. When prayer requests are in keeping with the Scriptures, one knows that the petition is according to God's will. The Bible is literally crammed to overflowing with examples of what God longs to give in answer to prayer.

Second, Paul has told us that

> Likewise the Spirit also helpeth with our infirmities: for we know not what we should pray for as we ought: but the Spirit itself maketh intercession for us with groanings which cannot be uttered. And he that searcheth the hearts knoweth what is the mind of the Spirit, because he maketh intercession for the saints according to the will of God (Rom. 8:26-27, KJV).

As we quiet ourselves before God, the Holy Spirit will speak and show us what to pray for. His inner witness is vital, because many specifics in our contemporary life-style are not individually dealt with in the Scriptures. This implies that prayer is never intended to be a mere monologue. Rather, it is a dialogue between God and ourselves. The Holy Spirit wishes to reveal what is in keeping with the mind of our Heavenly Father regarding every particular aspect of our daily lives. Therefore, we should always conclude our prayer by sincerely saying, "Nevertheless, not my will, but thine, be done" (Luke 22:42).

## Praying in Faith

One caution must be injected right here. To end prayer with the phrase "not my will, but thine, be done" must never be used as an easy out for failing to pray what the Bible calls *"the prayer of faith."* The Scriptures are very emphatic about this. The Epistle of James, for example, states: "Ask God . . . for God is a generous giver who neither refuses nor reproaches anyone. But he must ask in faith, without a doubt in his mind; for the doubter is like a heaving sea ruffled by the wind. A man of that kind must not expect the Lord to give him anything" (Jas. 1:6-7, NEB). God puts a high premium on faith as one prays. Our Lord went so far as to say, "If ye have faith as a grain of mustard seed, ye shall say to this mountain, Remove hence to yonder place; and it shall remove" (Matt. 17:20). Prayer can move mountains, but it must be the prayer of faith. Mountains of problems and difficulties can be removed by honest, faithful prayer.

Such faith is not easy to acquire, however. But remember the Bible promise quoted in an earlier chapter? Paul said, "So faith comes from what is heard, and what is heard comes by the preaching of Christ" (Rom. 10:17). Faith comes through meditating on the scriptural promises that relate to prayer, the character of Christ, and so on, and then becoming convinced that the things one asks for are in keeping with God's will. Bible meditation and praying in faith are inseparable.

We must be careful, however, not to put faith in prayer itself. The Heavenly Father is the object of true faith. There is no power in prayer as such. "Power belongs to God" (Ps. 62:11). Yet we can rely on the Holy Spirit; he will come to our aid and assist us to pray properly in faith if we have our hearts open to his inner work.

## Prayer in Jesus' Name

The Savior said, "I tell you, if you ask the Father for anything in my name, he will give it you. So far you have asked nothing in my name. Ask and you will receive, that your joy may be complete" (John 16:23-24, NEB). These verses emphasize the centrality of *praying in Jesus' name*. Of course, people usually end their prayers with that phrase or something like it. But far more is involved in our Lord's statement than just pinning a pious platitude on the end of our prayers out of mere habit or custom. What does it imply?

The heart of the principle lies in the truth that no one can come to God except in the righteousness of Jesus Christ. All are sinners. All are unclean. None are righteous, no not one. But Jesus Christ has made access to God possible by his death and resurrection. Through him believers are righteous and thus acceptable to the Father.

Therefore, when one prays it is vital to approach God humbly, not in one's own righteousness, but in the name and righteousness of the Lord and Savior Jesus Christ. Our prayers are acceptable only in him. To realize this truth and to be conscious of it are the essence of bold prayer (Heb. 4:16). It is not fervor, zeal, or even sincerity that makes prayers acceptable before a righteous and holy God, even though they have their place in prayer. Rather, it is praying in Jesus' name that permits the loving Father to hear and answer.

## Praying from a Pure Heart

The psalmist tells us, "If I regard iniquity in my heart, the Lord will not hear me" (Ps. 66:18, KJV). Perhaps the greatest hindrance to answered prayer is unconfessed sins. To harbor consciously some sin destroys vital fellowship with God. Prayer should, therefore, begin by quieting one's self before the Father, listening to the voice of the Spirit as he points out sin, and then honestly acknowledging the situation. As the Holy Spirit places his convicting finger on the evil, confessing and forsaking the sin is mandatory. When one has acknowledged with humility and sincerity every deviation from God's perfect will, the claim of forgiveness and cleansing can be made. The channel of communication then opens between one's self and God, and the assurance that he hears and answers is given. Confession and prevailing prayer are intrinsically united.

## The Summary

All that has been said concerning various elements of prayer can be summed up in the phrase, "praying . . . in the Spirit." Paul states Christians should find themselves "Praying always with all prayer and supplication in the Spirit" (Eph. 6:18, KJV). The Holy Spirit, as the Teacher in the school of prayer, instructs in the rudiments and the sophistications of prayer for effective intercession. He inspires faith, prays through the Christian, convicts of sin, and lifts one's very soul into the presence of the Savior. In summary, he is the one who makes prayer alive. This is praying "in the Spirit." All dynamic prayer is through the activity of the blessed Spirit of God. Therefore, it is essential to hear his voice as one prays and permit him to speak through the heart to God. In this manner prayer becomes a vital communication with the Father in heaven. What an adventure with the Spirit!

Prayer is essential to all genuine spiritual realities. No Christian can grow or serve Christ effectively or life in any manner pleasing to God apart from a vital, dynamic, growing, maturing, prayer life. If one is ever to be personally revived, the lesson of disciplined prayer must be learned. It cannot be repeated too often; the revived life emerges from and is permeated by a devoted life of prayer.

## Congregational Implications

The truths concerning prayer are not only applicable on an individual basis, they also have congregational implications. The church as a body of Christ should learn how to pray together. Oh, that there could be a dedicated and sacrificial prayer band in every congregation to seek God's reviving power upon the whole body of Christ. God is interested in far more than just reviving you as an individual, though he is certainly concerned for that. He longs to revive the entire church, the whole community, the expanse of the nation, even the whole world. God is constantly seeking those upon whom he can pour out his Spirit in awakening power. All that he waits upon is a praying people. *Prayer is the bottom line for any true spiritual awakening.* Dig down deep enough in any historical outpouring of the Spirit, and one discovers that prayer is always the basis of the moving of the Spirit of God. It was John Wesley who said: "Bear up the hands that hang down, by faith and prayer; support the tottering knees. Have you any dates of fasting and prayer? Storm the throne of grace and persevere therein, and mercy will come down." Whitefield confessed: "Whole days and weeks have I spent prostrate on the ground in silent or vocal prayer."

Through Wesley and Whitefield God gave one of the greatest revivals the church has ever witnessed. Prayer was central and vital in their movement.

## The Ultimate Question

Could it be that the real reason God is reviving you according to the principles laid out in this book is that he has in mind to make of you a prayer channel to precipitate a sweeping revival as well as experience a new touch of God on your individual life? Is it possible that God has something far more glorious in mind than you ever realized as you begin your journey toward a revived Christian life-style? The Holy Spirit hovers over every believer with a divine desire and holy hope that he can fashion that believer into a sincere prayer warrior. The world waits for interceding saints to pray down God's power upon a needy and godless society.

S. D. Gordon said,

> The greatest thing anyone can do for God and man is to pray. It is not the only thing. But it is the chief thing. . . . The great people of the earth to-day are the people who pray. I do not mean those who talk about prayer; nor those who say they believe in prayer; nor yet those who can explain about prayer; but I mean those people who *take* time and *pray*.[9]

How we need to pray in an unusual and sacrificial manner. As E. M. Bounds put it, "What the Church needs today is not more or better machinery, not new organizations or more and novel methods, but men whom the Holy Ghost can use—men of prayer, men mighty in prayer."[10]

Will you then join the intercessors? Will you, as a revived Christian, pray for a great awakening to dawn upon us? All that God is doing in your life may well be leading you to that end. Be a contributor. A revived life is a contributing life. And no contribution any Christian can make is greater than joining the ranks of the intercessors. Pray—get others to join you. Form a prayer group—it need not be large. Gather a few revived believers together and pray, pray, pray, until the awakening that God desires to send bursts upon you, your church, and your society. The world waits.

# Epilogue

I appeal to you therefore, brethren, by the mercies of God, to present your bodies as a living sacrifice, holy and acceptable to God, which is your spiritual worship. Do not be conformed to this world but be transformed by the renewal of your mind, that you may prove what is the will of God, what is good and acceptable and perfect (Rom. 12:1-2).

Christmas Evans was a man greatly used by God in revival. The Holy Spirit employed him to bring an awakening all over Wales. That was many years ago in the last century. It all began when he made what he called "A Solemn Covenant with God." It is found below. The closing challenge in this brief epilogue is to you, to read it carefully and prayerfully. Then, under God's leadership, make a similar covenant and sign it. It may be our Lord Jesus Christ will use this act of consecration to revive you mightily and then use you to help bring an awakening to others. May God enable you to give yourself to God in revival living and praying.

## A Solemn Covenant with God

I. I give my soul and body unto Thee, Jesus, the true God, and everlasting life; deliver us from sin, and from eternal death, and bring me into life everlasting. Amen.

II. I call the day, the sun, the earth, the trees, the stones, the bed, the table and the books, to witness that I come unto Thee, Redeemer of sinners, that I may obtain rest for my soul from the thunders of guilt and the dread of eternity. Amen.

III. I do, through confidence in Thy power, earnestly entreat Thee to take the work into Thine own hand, and give me a circumcised heart, that I may love Thee; and create in me a right spirit, that I may seek Thy glory. Grant me that principle which Thou wilt own in the day of judgment, that I may not then assume pale-facedness, and find myself a hypocrite. Grant me this, for the sake of Thy most precious blood. Amen.

IV. I entreat Thee, Jesus, the Son of God, in power, grant me, for the sake of Thy agonizing death, a covenant interest in Thy blood which cleanseth; in Thy righteousness, which justifieth; and in Thy redemption, which delivereth. I entreat an interest in Thy blood, for Thy blood's sake, and a part in Thee, for Thy name's sake, which Thou has given among men. Amen.

V. O Jesus Christ, Son of the living God, take for the sake of Thy cruel death, my time, and strength, and the gifts and talents I possess; which, with a full purpose of heart, I consecrate to Thy glory in the building up of Thy Church in the world, for Thou art worthy of the hearts and talents of men. Amen.

VI. I desire Thee, my great High Priest, to confirm, by Thy power from Thy High Court, my usefulness as a preacher, and my piety as a Christian, as two gardens nigh to each other; that sin may not have place in my heart to becloud my confidence in Thy righteousness, and that I may not be left to any foolish act that may occasion my gifts to wither, and I be rendered useless before my life ends. Keep Thy gracious eye upon me, and watch over me, O my Lord, and my God for ever! Amen.

VII. I give myself in a particular manner to Thee, O Jesus Christ the Saviour, to be preserved from the falls into which many stumble, that Thy name (in Thy cause) may not be blasphemed or wounded, that my peace may not be injured, and that Thy people may not be grieved, and that Thine enemies may not be hardened. Amen.

VIII. I come entreating Thee to enter into a covenant with me in my ministry. Oh, prosper me as Thou didst prosper Bunyan, Vavasor, Powell, Howell Harris, Rowlands, and Whitefield. The impediments in the way of my prosperity remove. Work in me the things approved of God that I may attain this. Give me a heart "sick of love" to Thee, and to the souls of men. Grant that I may feel the power of Thy Word before preaching it, as Moses felt the power of his rod before he felt the effect of it on the land and waters of Egypt. For the sake of Thy precious blood, Jesus, my all in all, grant me this. Amen.

IX. Search me now, and lead me in the paths of judgment. May I see in this world what I really am in Thy sight, that I may not find myself otherwise when the light of eternity shall dawn upon me, and open my eyes in the brightness of immortality. Wash me in Thy redeeming blood. Amen.

X. Give me power to trust in Thee for food and raiment, and make known my requests to Thee. O let Thy care be over me as a covenant privilege betwixt Thee and me, and not simply as a general care which Thou shewest in feeding the ravens that perish and clothing the lily that is cast into the oven, but remember me as one of Thy family, and as one of Thy unworthy brethren. Amen.

XI. Take upon Thyself, O Jesus, to prepare me for death, for Thou art God; and Thou needest but to speak the word. If it be possible—but Thy will be done—let me not linger in sickness, nor die a sudden death without bidding adieu to my brethren, but rather let me die with them around me, after a short illness. May everything be put in order ready for that day of passing from one world to another, so that there may be no confusion or disorder, but a passing away in peace. O grant me this for the sake of Thine agony in the garden. Amen.

XII. Grant, O blessed Lord, that no sin may be nourished or fostered in me which may cause Thee to cast me off from the work of Thy sanctuary, like the sons of Eli; and, for the sake of Thine infinite merits, let not my days be longer than my usefulness. Let me not become, at the end of my days, like a piece of lumber in the way of the usefulness of others. Amen.

XIII. I beseech Thee, my Redeemer, to present these supplications of mine before the Father; and oh, inscribe them in Thy book with Thine own immortal pen, while I am writing them with my mortal hand in my book on earth. According to the depths of Thy merit, and Thy infinite grace, and Thy compassion, and Thy tenderness toward Thy people, O attach Thy name in Thine Upper Court to these humble supplications of mine; and set Thine amen to them, even as I set mine on my side of the covenant. Amen.

Signed: _____

# Notes

**Foreword**

1. Norman P. Grubb, *Continuous Revival* (Ft. Washington, Pennsylvania: Christian Literature Crusade, 1975), p. 6.

**Chapter 1**

1. John Wesley, *The Journal of the Rev. John Wesley, A.M.*, ed. Nehemiah Curnock (London: Epworth Press, 1938), 1:475-76.
2. Ibid., 2:121-25.
3. Charles G. Finney, *Memoirs of Rev. Charles G. Finney* (New York: Fleming H. Revell, 1876), pp. 12-18.
4. Ibid., pp. 18-23.
5. See James Burns, *Revivals: Their Laws and Leaders* (London: Hodder and Stoughton, 1909).
6. Charles G. Finney, *Lectures on Revivals of Religion* (New York: Fleming H. Revell, 1868), p. 23.

**Chapter 3**

1. Bertha Smith, *Go Home and Tell* (Nashville: Broadman Press, 1965), pp. 14-17.

**Chapter 4**

1. James Gilchrist Lawson, *Deeper Experiences of Famous Christians* (Anderson, Indiana: The Warner Press, 1911), p. 346
2. Ibid., pp. 373-74 (edited).
3. R. A. Torrey, *The Holy Spirit: Who He Is and What He Does and How to Know Him in All the Fulness of His Gracious and Glorious Ministry* (New York: Fleming H. Revell, 1927), p. 198.
4. W. H. Griffith Thomas, *The Holy Spirit of God*, 3rd ed. (Grand Rapids, Michigan: Wm. B. Eerdmans, 1955), pp. 196-97.

## Chapter 5

1. Steven Barabas, *So Great Salvation* (New York: Fleming H. Revell), pp. 88-89.
2. Evan H. Hopkins, *The Law of Liberty in the Spiritual Life* (Philadelphia: Sunday School Times, 1955), p. 108.
3. Rosalind Rinker, *Prayer: Conversing with God* (Grand Rapids, Michigan: Zondervan Press, 1959), p. 22.

## Chapter 6

1. Quoted in Lawson, *Deeper Experiences*, p. 102.
2. F. B. Meyer, *Peace, Perfect Peace* (New York: Fleming H. Revell, 1897), pp. 7-8.
3. Oswald Chambers, *My Utmost for His Highest* (New York: Dodd, Mead, & Company, 1954), p. 81.
4. Miles Stanford, *Principles of Spiritual Growth* (Lincoln, Nebraska: Back to the Bible Broadcast, 1969), pp. 62-63.

## Chapter 7

1. John R. W. Stott, *Our Guilty Silence* (London: Hodder and Stoughton, 1967), p. 25.
2. John R. W. Stott, *One People* (London: Falcon Books, 1969), p. 24.
3. Marcus Dods, *The First Epistle to the Corinthians*, *The Expositor's Bible* (London: Hodder and Stoughton, 1891), p. 276.
4. Archibald Robertson and Alfred Plummer, *A Critical and Exegetical Commentary on the First Epistle of St. Paul to the Corinthians*, *The International Critical Commentary* (Edinburgh: T. & T. Clark, 1953), p. 264.
5. Alexander Rattray Hay, *The New Testament Order for Church and Missionary* (New Testament Missionary Union, 1947), p. 177.
6. Ibid., p. 186.
7. William Barclay, *The Letters to the Corinthians* (Edinburgh: St. Andrew Press, 1954), p. 124.
8. Samuel Chadwick as quoted by Leonard Ravenhill, *Revival Praying* (Minneapolis: Bethany Fellowship, Inc., 1962), p. 440.
9. S. D. Gordon, *Quiet Talks on Prayer* (New York: Grosset & Dunlap, 1904), p. 12.
10. Quoted in Leonard Ravenhill, *A Treasury of Prayer* (Minneapolis: Bethany Fellowship, Inc., 1961), p. 89.